RxPrep®

Part of the UWorld Family

7ᵀᴴ EDITION CALIFORNIA LAW SUMMARY FOR CPJE

Law, Pharmacy Administration & Exam-Specific Items

Editors

Tessa Overman, PharmD, BCPS, BCCP

Chelsea Bombatch, PharmD, BCPS

Stephanie Garrett, PharmD, BCPS

Caitlin Davis, PharmD, BCPS

Associate Editors

Stephanie Brian, PharmD, BCPS

Faith Wellings, PharmD, BCPS

Lauren Devine, PharmD, BCPS, BCCP

Primary Sources

Food and Drug Administration, at www.fda.gov

National Association of Boards of Pharmacy, at https://nabp.pharmacy

DEA's Pharmacist's Manual, at www.deadiversion.usdoj.gov/pubs/manuals

U.S. Pharmacopeia Chapters, at www.usp.org

WELCOME TO THE 7ᵀᴴ EDITION RxPREP

CPJE EXAM
REVIEW

Welcome to RxPrep's California Practice Standards and Jurisprudence Examination for Pharmacists (CPJE) review. This Manual is intended to be used with RxPrep's CPJE online Video Lectures and Test Banks, which correlate with the topics in this Manual. The course is intended to be used in this manner:

- Read this Manual and watch the Video Lectures.

- Test yourself with the corresponding Test Bank. Each Test Bank question should be known prior to testing, with an understanding of why the answer is correct. This will permit correct responses to similar items, worded differently, that you may find on the actual exam.

- Take the RxPrep CPJE Practice Exam to test your retention and feel confident on exam day.

Please visit the RxPrep website at www.rxprep.com to find a study method that has worked well for many other CPJE test takers, as well as other resources.

The majority of questions on the CPJE involve the practical drug knowledge expected of a newly-licensed pharmacist in a community or hospital pharmacy. To perform well on the CPJE, the RxPrep CPJE Course and the NAPLEX Course should be used together. The NAPLEX Course includes the topics that overlap in both exams. This CPJE Course covers:

- Clinical items that are not included with the NAPLEX course (e.g., therapeutic interchange, formulary management, physical assessments, health screenings and medication utilization evaluation).

- The required aspects of federal law (e.g., DEA requirements for controlled substances).

- The detailed pharmacy law for California.

We wish you the best for your CPJE preparation.

The RxPrep Team
www.rxprep.com

Acknowledgements

The editors would like to acknowledge the expertise and vision of Karen Shapiro, PharmD, BCPS for developing the original framework and content of the RxPrep CPJE materials.

Contributors

Amy Drew, PharmD, BCPS

Mindy Holcombe, PharmD, BCPS, BCPPS

Bobbie Varghese, PharmD

Angie Veverka, PharmD, BCPS

Joni Hutton – graphic design and production

Dacy Lim – proofing and editorial services

Michelle Sinfield, Liliana Urquizo – editorial services

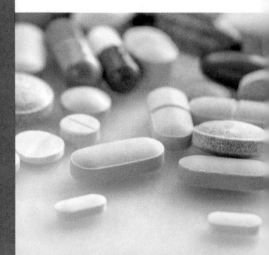

TABLE OF CONTENTS

CHAPTER 1

PAGE 1

INTRODUCTION TO THE **CALIFORNIA PRACTICE STANDARDS AND JURISPRUDENCE EXAM**

CHAPTER 2

PAGE 5

PHARMACY OPERATIONS

CHAPTER 3

PAGE 28

PHARMACY PRACTICE PART 1: PRESCRIBING AND DISPENSING

CHAPTER 4

PAGE 65

PHARMACY PRACTICE PART 2: FURNISHING, ADMINISTERING AND CLINICAL SERVICES

CHAPTER 5

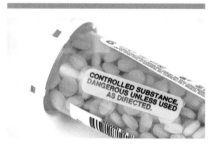

PAGE 93

CONTROLLED SUBSTANCES PART 1: THE CONTROLLED SUBSTANCES ACT

CHAPTER 6

PAGE 101

CONTROLLED SUBSTANCES PART 2: ORDERING AND DISPOSAL

CHAPTER 7

PAGE 115

CONTROLLED SUBSTANCES PART 3: PRESCRIBING AND DISPENSING

CHAPTER 8

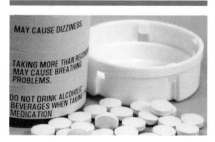

PAGE 135

AUXILIARY LABELS

PAGE 141

INDEX

INTRODUCTION TO THE
CALIFORNIA PRACTICE STANDARDS AND JURISPRUDENCE EXAM

CHAPTER CONTENTS

California Practice Standards and Jurisprudence Exam 2
   What is Unique About CPJE? 2
Supplemental Resources 3
Format of the CPJE 3
CPJE Content Outline 4
How to Prepare for CPJE Using RxPrep 4

INTRODUCTION TO THE
CALIFORNIA PRACTICE STANDARDS AND JURISPRUDENCE EXAM

CALIFORNIA PRACTICE STANDARDS AND JURISPRUDENCE EXAM

To become licensed as a pharmacist in California, an applicant must pass two exams:

- The North American Pharmacist Licensure Examination (NAPLEX®), which is administered by the National Association of Boards of Pharmacy (NABP).

- The California Practice Standards and Jurisprudence Examination for Pharmacists (CPJE), which is administered by the California State Board of Pharmacy. The Multistate Pharmacy Jurisprudence Exam (MPJE®) is not required for licensure in California.

Applicants will find helpful information on the "Applicants" page of the California State Board of Pharmacy website.[1] The CPJE PSI Candidate Information Bulletin reviews the composition of the exam, the content outline, sample questions and more.[2]

WHAT IS UNIQUE ABOUT CPJE?

Although the CPJE is considered a law exam, a vast majority of the questions are clinical in nature. Applicants with a high NAPLEX score (e.g., triple digits) generally feel comfortable with the clinical content of the CPJE, but it is critical to study clinical content for CPJE in addition to California law.

Use This Manual with the RxPrep NAPLEX Course

Any information in the RxPrep NAPLEX Course can be tested on the CPJE, including calculations (e.g., flow rates, creatinine clearance calculations, compounding calculations and others). Information in these topics may be especially important: Infectious Diseases I – IV, HIV, Immunizations, Travelers, Medication Safety & Quality Improvement, Acute & Critical Care Medicine and Learning IV Medications. To master brand/generic names of top selling drugs, the RxPrep NAPLEX Top Sellers Test Banks should be thoroughly reviewed.

---

1   https://www.pharmacy.ca.gov/applicants/rph.shtml (accessed 2020 Nov 13)
2   https://candidate.psiexams.com/bulletin/display_bulletin.jsp?ro=yes&actionname=83&bulletinid=230&bulletinurl=.pdf (accessed 2020 Nov 13)

The RxPrep California Law Summary for CPJE is specifically tailored for the <u>law</u> portion of the CPJE. This Manual covers some clinical topics that are important for CPJE that are not covered in the RxPrep NAPLEX Course (e.g., several pharmacist-provided clinical services authorized under SB 493, drug formularies, therapeutic interchange, standard order sets and medication utilization evaluation).

RxPrep recommends taking the CPJE no later than 2 – 3 weeks after the NAPLEX in order to retain the drug information you learned for the NAPLEX. Some students will take the CPJE first due to scheduling conflicts, and this is usually fine.

SUPPLEMENTAL RESOURCES

Additional recommended resources for the CPJE include:

- The California Pharmacy Lawbook which includes pharmacy-related regulations from the Business and Professions Code (B&PC), California Code of Regulations (CCR) and Health and Safety Code (H&SC).[3] Key regulations are referenced in this manual for the applicant who wishes to look them up.
- Previous issues of the board's newsletter, _The Script_.[4]
- Published monographs on drug therapy called _Health Notes_ (if available).
- <u>Community Pharmacy and Hospital Outpatient Pharmacy Self-Assessment Form</u>.[5]

The <u>Self-Assessment Forms</u> are completed by the pharmacist-in-charge for every California-licensed pharmacy, by July 1st of each odd-numbered year. The forms are developed by the California State Board of Pharmacy as a tool to ensure that the pharmacy is following all the legal requirements for operations. The <u>Compounding Self-Assessment Form</u> is also helpful for the exam. Items from the Self-Assessment Forms are reviewed in this Manual and tested in the CPJE Test Banks.

Pharmacy law constantly changes. Before sitting for the exam, check the California State Board of Pharmacy website for updates.

FORMAT OF THE CPJE

The CPJE is a <u>2-hour exam</u> with <u>90 multiple-choice questions</u>. Of the 90 questions, 75 questions count towards the score. The other 15 questions are pre-test questions that are being evaluated for inclusion on future exams. The pre-test questions are distributed throughout the exam and do not affect the score. It is not possible to change an answer once the answer choice is confirmed and you have moved to the next question. There is only one answer for each question. Since scores on the examination are based on the number of correct answers, there is no penalty for guessing. It is to your advantage to answer every question.

---

3   https://www.pharmacy.ca.gov/laws_regs/lawbook (accessed 2020 Nov 13)
4   https://www.pharmacy.ca.gov/publications/script.shtml (accessed 2020 Nov 13)
5   https://www.pharmacy.ca.gov/licensees/facility/self_assess.shtml (accessed 2020 Nov 13)

CPJE scores are mailed to the applicant's address of record about 30 days after the exam. The board occasionally conducts a quality assurance (QA) assessment to ensure that the exam questions are appropriate. Scores may be delayed for applicants testing during a QA period.

CPJE CONTENT OUTLINE

The Content Outline for CPJE can be found in the CPJE Candidate Information Bulletin. After you register to take the CPJE, the Bulletin will be sent to you in the mail. CPJE content is divided into the following three areas:

- Patient Medications (20 items or ~27% of the scored questions)
- Patient Outcomes (33 items or ~44% of the scored questions)
    - This area covers clinical content such as developing a therapeutic regimen, performing monitoring, resolving problems (e.g., adverse drug events, drug interactions), initiating pharmacist-provider therapies and many others. Refer to the RxPrep NAPLEX Course as needed.
- Pharmacy Operations (22 items or ~29% of the scored questions)

HOW TO PREPARE FOR CPJE USING RxPREP

Use your time wisely and create a study plan. Remember, any content in the RxPrep NAPLEX Course can be tested on CPJE. Review brand and generic names of top selling drugs and make sure the indication and common safety issues are known. Practice reviewing patient profiles and decide if the drug to be dispensed is safe and appropriate for the patient.

Make sure that you are well-prepared prior to testing. Do not test until you have:

LAW STUDY TIP

- The Law Study Tip highlights important information for testing.
- The tips may include practice scenarios or provide a way to organize the information.

- Read the RxPrep CPJE Manual and watched the Video Lectures. Key information will be underlined throughout the CPJE Manual. Law Study Tips are used throughout the Manual to highlight important points.
- Reviewed the items on the Self-Assessment Forms for (minimally) Community Pharmacy and Hospital Outpatient and Compounding. Pretend you are the pharmacist-in-charge and complete these.
- Reviewed the practice questions in the CPJE PSI Candidate Information Bulletin.
- Reviewed necessary clinical content from the RxPrep NAPLEX Course, including top selling brand/generic names.
- Completed the RxPrep CPJE Test Bank questions (and understand why the answers are correct).
- Scored well on the RxPrep CPJE Practice Exam.

CHAPTER 2

PHARMACY OPERATIONS

CHAPTER CONTENTS

California Board of Pharmacy 6
Duties and Licensure of the Pharmacy Staff 6
Pharmacist-in-Charge 7
Pharmacist 7
Advanced Practice Pharmacist 10
Intern Pharmacist 10
Pharmacy Technician 11
Pharmacy Technician Trainee 12
Pharmacy Clerk 12
Pharmacist Recovery Program for Substance Abuse and Mental Illness 12
Inspection of a Pharmacy 13
Facility and Equipment Requirements 13
Pharmacy Security 14
Policies and Procedures 14
Recordkeeping and Reporting Requirements 15
Paper Prescription Recordkeeping System for Controlled Substances 17
DEA Controlled Substances Inventory 17
Off-Site Storage of Records 18
Order Requirements for Supplying and Billing Durable Medical Equipment 19
Drug Pedigrees 20
Delivery of Drugs to a Pharmacy 21
Drug Stock 22
Adulteration and Misbranding 22
Monthly Inspection of Drug Supply 23
Drug and Vaccine Shortages 23
Drug Storage 23
Drug Supply at Nursing Stations 23
Drug Recalls 24
Return, Disposal or Reuse of Drugs 25
Pharmacies Donating Drugs for Redistribution 25
Patients Returning or Disposing of Drugs 25
Mandatory Reporting of Abuse and Neglect 27

CHAPTER 2
PHARMACY OPERATIONS

This section reviews California law for dispensing prescriptions and primarily covers non-controlled substances. Regulations for controlled substances are more stringent and are reviewed separately.

CALIFORNIA BOARD OF PHARMACY

The board's vision statement is "Healthy Californians through quality pharmacist's care."

The board protects and promotes the health and safety of Californians by pursuing the highest quality of pharmacist's care and the appropriate use of pharmaceuticals through education, communication, licensing, legislation, regulation and enforcement.

The board includes 13 members, each of whom serves 1 or 2 four-year terms. The board elects a president, a vice president and a treasurer. The board may appoint an executive officer, who may (or may not) be a board member.

The board oversees all aspects of pharmacy practice, including pharmacies, pharmacy staff and products (drugs and devices). Additionally, the board regulates drug wholesalers and other facilities that store and furnish prescription drugs. Pharmacy inspectors work for the board and ensure legal compliance with the pharmacy laws. They have the power to arrest, without a warrant, a person who they believe has violated the pharmacy laws.

DUTIES AND LICENSURE OF THE PHARMACY STAFF

Pharmacists, interns, pharmacy technicians and pharmacy technician trainees must wear <u>name tags</u> when at work, in 18-point type, that contain their <u>name</u> and <u>license status</u>.[6] All licensees <u>must</u> also join the <u>board's email notification list</u> within 60 days of becoming licensed.[7]

---

6 B&PC 680, B&PC 4115.5(e), CCR 1793.7(c)
7 B&PC 4013(d)

PHARMACIST-IN-CHARGE

Each pharmacy must have a pharmacist-in-charge (PIC) who is responsible for the daily operations of the pharmacy. The PIC has authority to make sure that the pharmacy is compliant with both federal and state law. The PIC has <u>strict liability</u> for violation of the law in the pharmacy, even if he or she did not have actual knowledge of the violation. The PIC can supervise up to <u>two pharmacies</u> as long as they are within <u>50 driving miles</u> of each other.[8] Any <u>change of PIC</u> must be <u>reported</u> by the pharmacy and the departing PIC to the board <u>in writing within 30 days</u>. A pharmacist cannot serve as the PIC of a pharmacy and a Designated Representative-In-Charge (DRIC) for a wholesaler or a veterinary food-animal drug retailer at the same time.

The PIC must complete a <u>biennial</u> (i.e., every other year) <u>Self-Assessment form</u> for their pharmacy <u>before July 1 of each odd numbered year</u> (e.g., by July 1, 2021, then again by July 1, 2023). An additional Self-Assessment form must be completed within <u>30 days</u> if a <u>new permit</u> is issued, when the pharmacy has a <u>new PIC</u> and when the pharmacy moves to a <u>new location</u>. Each Self-Assessment form will be kept in the pharmacy for <u>three years</u>. The Self-Assessment form is not sent to anyone, but if the pharmacy is visited by an inspector they will need to produce the form and the inspector will compare the actual situation in the pharmacy to what is on the form.

PHARMACIST

The traditional role of a pharmacist is the safe and proper dispensing of medications. The pharmacist receives new prescriptions, interprets the prescriptions, interprets the clinical data in the patient's medication records, consults with other healthcare professionals, performs drug utilization reviews (DURs), provides counseling and supervises the pharmacy staff.

© Dragon Images/Shutterstock.com

To be licensed as a pharmacist, a candidate must have:[9]

- Reached the age of 18 years or older.
- Graduated from an Accreditation Council for Pharmacy Education (ACPE)-accredited school of pharmacy or be a graduate of a foreign school of pharmacy and be certified by the National Association of Boards of Pharmacy (NABP)'s Foreign Pharmacy Graduate Examination Committee (FPGEC).
- Completed at least 150 hours of semester college credit, 90 of which must be from a pharmacy school. The candidate must also have earned at least a baccalaureate degree in a course of study devoted to pharmacy.
- Completed <u>1,500 hours of pharmacy practice experience</u>.
  - ❏ Candidates who graduated from an <u>ACPE-accredited school of pharmacy</u> after January 1, 2016 are deemed to have satisfied the pharmacy practice experience hours.[10]
  - ❏ Foreign graduates and those who graduated prior to January 1, 2016, must complete 1,500 intern hours within the United States. A Pharmacy Intern Hours Affidavit is required and must document experience in both community and institutional settings.[11]

8   CCR 1709.1
9   B&PC 4200
10   B&PC 4209
11   https://www.pharmacy.ca.gov/forms/rph_app_pkt.pdf (accessed 2020 Nov 13)

- Passed the NAPLEX and CPJE. A person who has failed the CPJE 4 times will need to enroll in an ACPE-accredited school of pharmacy in order to complete 16 semester units of additional coursework in pharmacy before they are able to retake the exam.
- Passed a criminal background check.

If a licensee in another state moves to California because their partner is stationed here with a division of the United States Armed Forces, the board will expedite the licensure process.

Under California law, all registered pharmacists (RPhs) can provide the following services after meeting certain training requirements:[12]

- Administer drugs and biologics when ordered by a prescriber. Previously, pharmacists were permitted to administer only oral and topical drugs. Pharmacists can now administer drugs by other routes, including by injection.
- Provide consultation, training and education about drug therapy, disease management and disease prevention.
- Participate in multidisciplinary reviews of patient progress, which includes appropriate access to medical records.
- Furnish self-administered hormonal contraceptives, which includes oral formulations (birth control pills), transdermal (patch) and vaginal (ring) preparations and injections.
- Furnish travel medications recommended by the CDC and which do not require a diagnosis.
- Furnish prescription nicotine replacement products for smoking cessation, including the inhaler (such as *Nicotrol)* and the nasal spray (such as *Nicotrol NS)*.
- Independently initiate and administer immunizations recommended by the CDC to patients three years of age and older. A physician protocol is still required to administer immunizations to children younger than three years old.
- Order and interpret tests for the purpose of monitoring and managing the efficacy and toxicity of drug therapies, in coordination with the patient's primary care provider (PCP) or with the diagnosing prescriber.

Continuing Education and License Renewal

In order to ensure that pharmacists are up-to-date with new drug changes and treatment guidelines, 30 hours of continuing education (CE) must be completed during each two-year license period.[13] For license renewals on or after July 1, 2019, at least two hours of pharmacy law and ethics must be included with each renewal. The license expires on the last day of the pharmacist's birth month. The first two-year license cycle is exempt from CE requirements since the pharmacist is considered up to date. The certificate of completion of CEs must be kept for four years.

Pharmacists must disclose (on the renewal form) if any government agency issued disciplinary action against any of their licenses that resulted in a restriction or penalty being placed on the license, such as revocation, suspension, probation, public reprimand or reproval. Pharmacists must disclose on the license renewal form if they have been convicted of any violation of law,

12   B&PC 4052
13   CCR 1732.5

except for traffic violations that do not involve <u>alcohol</u> or <u>controlled substances</u>. Electronic fingerprints must be on file with the board.[14]

Pharmacist Breaks

It is common in smaller pharmacies for there to be only one pharmacist on duty, and if the pharmacist leaves for a break, there will be no pharmacist present. In such a case, the pharmacist can leave the pharmacy for breaks and meal periods for <u>up to 30 minutes</u>. The pharmacy can stay open and the pharmacist does not need to stay in the pharmacy area during the break. The ancillary staff (i.e., intern pharmacists, pharmacy technicians, clerks) can stay in the pharmacy if the pharmacist believes that the drugs and devices will be <u>secure</u> when he or she is gone. During this time, the staff can continue to perform <u>non-discretionary duties</u>. "Non-discretionary" means that the work does not include making decisions that require clinical judgment. Non-discretionary tasks are routine and repetitive, and include removing drugs from stock, counting, pouring or mixing pharmaceuticals, placing the product into containers and applying the label to a prescription bottle.

Interns cannot counsel patients when there is no pharmacist to supervise. Any duty performed by other staff members must be reviewed by the pharmacist upon his or her return to the pharmacy. While the pharmacist is away, only <u>refill</u> medications that the pharmacist has already checked and which do not require patient counseling can be dispensed.[15]

A law passed in 2018 <u>prohibits</u> a <u>community</u> pharmacy from <u>requiring</u> a pharmacist to <u>work alone</u>. It requires that another employee of either the pharmacy or the establishment be made available to assist the pharmacist at all times, with some exceptions.[16]

Staff That Pharmacists Can Supervise

PHARMACIST SUPERVISION LIMITS

The maximum numbers of staff that a pharmacist can supervise are as follows:

Interns: two per pharmacist

Technicians, Community Setting: the first pharmacist may supervise one technician; each additional pharmacist may supervise two technicians

Technicians, Hospital Setting: two per pharmacist

Technician Trainees: one per pharmacist for a 120–140 hour training period; if the trainee's externship involves a rotation between community and hospital pharmacy, the externship can be up to 340 hours in total

Clerks: a reasonable number, at each pharmacist's discretion

---

14 CCR 1702
15 B&PC 1714.1
16 B&PC 4113.5

ADVANCED PRACTICE PHARMACIST

The advanced practice pharmacist (APh) license enables pharmacists to provide clinical services in various settings. The role of an APh is similar to that of clinical pharmacists in a hospital or ambulatory care setting. Historically, and in the absence of provider status, clinical services have been performed under a collaborative practice agreement (CPA) or protocol.

APhs can do the following:[17]

- Perform patient assessments.
- Order and interpret drug therapy-related tests in coordination with the patient's PCP or with the diagnosing prescriber.
- Refer patients to other healthcare providers.
- Participate in the evaluation and management of diseases and health conditions in collaboration with other healthcare providers.
- Initiate, adjust and discontinue drug therapy pursuant to an order by a patient's treating prescriber and in accordance with established protocols. If the APh is initiating or adjusting a controlled substance, the APh must be registered with the Drug Enforcement Administration (DEA).

In order to be recognized as an APh, a pharmacist must meet two of the three following requirements:[18]

- Earn certification in a relevant area of practice, such as ambulatory care, critical care, oncology pharmacy or pharmacotherapy.[19,20,21]
- Complete a postgraduate residency program.
- Have provided clinical services to patients for one year (and at least 1,500 hours) under a CPA or protocol with a physician, an APh, a pharmacist practicing Collaborative Drug Therapy Management (CDTM) or within a health system.[22]

In order to maintain the APh designation, the pharmacist must pay a renewal fee and provide proof of completion of 10 hours of CE per cycle. These hours are in addition to the 30 hours required for the pharmacist license. The APh is exempt from the CE requirement in the first renewal cycle.

INTERN PHARMACIST

An intern pharmacist can perform almost all functions of a pharmacist at the discretion and under the supervision of a pharmacist. An intern pharmacist cannot have a key to the pharmacy. All prescriptions filled by an intern pharmacist must be checked by a pharmacist before dispensing.[23]

---

17 B&PC 4052.6
18 B&PC 4210
19 CCR 1730.2
20 http://appharmacist.com/ (accessed 2020 Nov 13)
21 http://www.cshp.org/page/Certificate_Programs (accessed 2020 Nov 13)
22 CCR 1730.1(a)(3)
23 CCR 1717(b)(1)

In order to be registered as an intern pharmacist, the candidate must meet one of the following requirements:[24]

- Be currently enrolled as a student in a pharmacy school that is ACPE-accredited or which is recognized by the board.

- Be a graduate of a school of pharmacy that is ACPE-accredited or which is recognized by the board and who also has an application pending to become licensed as a pharmacist in California.

- Be a graduate of a foreign pharmacy school who has obtained certification from NABP's FPGEC. This is obtained after passing an English competency test (TOEFL) and the Foreign Pharmacy Graduate Equivalency Examination (FPGEE).

PHARMACY TECHNICIAN

Pharmacy technicians assist pharmacists with dispensing prescription drugs. In California, technicians are permitted to perform packaging, manipulative, repetitive or other <u>non-discretionary tasks</u> under the direct supervision of a pharmacist.[25]

makasana photo/Shutterstock.com

Outpatient prescriptions filled by a pharmacy technician must be checked by a pharmacist. In the hospital setting, technicians can check the work of other technicians, as described below. Each pharmacy must have job descriptions for the pharmacy technicians that work at that location, and written Policies and Procedures (P&Ps) to ensure compliance with California's legal requirements.

Tech-Check-Tech Programs

Pharmacy technicians who have received specialized training can participate in a tech-check-tech (TCT) program in <u>hospital</u> settings.[26] After a technician has finished filling or replenishing the <u>unit-dose distribution system, floor stock or ward stock</u>, another technician (instead of a pharmacist) can check the accuracy of the work. The TCT program is permitted only in acute care hospitals that have an ongoing <u>clinical pharmacy program</u>, and which have <u>pharmacists located in the patient care areas</u>. "Prescriptions" in acute care facilities are called medication

Tyler Olson/Shutterstock.com

orders, and the medication orders must have been verified by the pharmacist. The technicians involved with TCT cannot approve the orders; they can only confirm the accuracy of the filling.

A pharmacist must check <u>compounded</u> and <u>repackaged</u> drugs before a technician uses them to fill unit-dose distribution systems and floor/ward stock. The pharmacy must have a description of the hospital's clinical program on file before starting a TCT program. The PIC will need to carefully monitor the program to ensure that the requirements outlined in the hospital's TCT P&Ps are in place. A pharmacy technician assigned to this activity must have received specialized training, which will be outlined in the TCT P&Ps.

---

24   B&PC 4208
25   B&PC 4115
26   B&PC 1739.8

Technician Licensure

An individual can become licensed as a pharmacy technician if he or she is a high school graduate or possesses a general educational development (GED) certificate equivalent, and meets any one of the following requirements:[27]

- Obtained an associate's degree in pharmacy technology.
- Completed a course of training specified by the board.
- Graduated from a school of pharmacy recognized by the board.
- Completed a board-approved certification program accredited by the National Commission for Certifying Agencies including the Pharmacy Technician Certification Board (PTCB) and the National Healthcareer Association (NHA) programs.

PHARMACY TECHNICIAN TRAINEE

A pharmacy technician trainee is a person who is required to complete an externship as part of their educational program to become a pharmacy technician. The purpose of the externship is to gain practical training experience. The externship can be up to a total of 340 hours, with no more than 140 hours in any single rotation. The trainee will be able to perform non-discretionary tasks, which must be under the direct supervision of a pharmacist.[28]

PHARMACY CLERK

A non-licensed person (clerk/typist) can type a prescription label and enter prescription information into a computer, and request and receive refill authorizations.[29] A clerk is not allowed to pull drugs from the shelf or fill prescription medications. However, clerks can <u>put drugs on the shelf</u> and <u>give patients their prescriptions</u> at the point of transaction. There are <u>no maximum limits</u> on the number of clerks allowed to be in the pharmacy at one time. There can be as many clerks as the pharmacist feels that he or she can reasonably supervise.

📷 *all_about_people/Shutterstock.com*

PHARMACIST RECOVERY PROGRAM FOR SUBSTANCE ABUSE AND MENTAL ILLNESS

A past study indicated that 46% of pharmacists and 62% of pharmacy interns admitted to using controlled substances at some time without a valid prescription.[30] The pharmacists' greater access to drugs increases the risk for substance abuse. The board contracts with *Maximus, Inc.* to provide confidential assessment, referral and monitoring services for the Pharmacists Recovery Program.[31] The purpose of the program is to evaluate the drug abuse and/or mental illness, develop a treatment plan, monitor progress and provide support. The individual receives the help to recover and, if possible, returns to practicing pharmacy.

---

27 B&PC 4202
28 B&PC 4115.5
29 CCR 1793.3
30 https://pubmed.ncbi.nlm.nih.gov/2882673/ (accessed 2020 Nov 13)
31 http://www.pharmacy.ca.gov/licensees/personal/pharmacist_recovery.shtml (accessed 2020 Nov 13)

The Pharmacy Recovery Program accepts referrals on a <u>voluntary basis</u>. Any pharmacist or intern in California who is experiencing alcohol or other drug abuse or mental illness can seek assistance by contacting a 24-hour toll-free number. All voluntary requests for information and assistance are confidential and are not subject to discovery or subpoena. Family, friends, employers and colleagues are encouraged to contact the program for assistance.

The pharmacy must have a procedure in place for when a licensed pharmacy staff member is found to be chemically, mentally or physically impaired to the extent it affects his or her ability to practice, or is found to have engaged in the theft, diversion or self-use of drugs. If a pharmacist suspects another pharmacist is impaired at work, they must report this to the board within <u>14 days</u>.

The board also uses the program for pharmacists who are chemically dependent or mentally impaired. The board may <u>refer a pharmacist to the recovery program in lieu of discipline</u> if there has been no other significant violation of the pharmacy law. In cases that involve a serious violation, the board may refer a pharmacist to the program in addition to taking disciplinary action.

INSPECTION OF A PHARMACY

Board inspectors assess if pharmacies are compliant with federal and state laws and regulations. The pharmacy can face disciplinary actions if legal requirements are not met, including completion of the Self-Assessment form. An action plan must be noted to correct any non-compliance. The form is not sent anywhere but kept on file in the pharmacy in case an inspector wants to see it. There is a Self-Assessment form for different practice settings: community pharmacy/hospital outpatient, compounding and hospital inpatient. These Self-Assessment forms are important to review for practice and for the exam.

FACILITY AND EQUIPMENT REQUIREMENTS

The board has requirements for the pharmacy practice site, which include:

- An unobstructed area of adequate size for the safe practice of pharmacy.
- A sink with hot and cold running water.
- A readily accessible restroom.
- A suitable area for confidential patient consultation.
- Safeguards in place to prevent the theft of drugs and devices.
- The pharmacy premises, fixtures and equipment must be kept in a clean and orderly condition, properly lighted and free from rodents and insects.
- The original board-issued <u>pharmacy license</u> and the <u>current renewal</u> must be posted where they can be <u>clearly read</u> by the public.[32]

---

32 B&PC 4058

There are additional requirements if the pharmacy compounds sterile drugs:

- The pharmacy maintains written documentation regarding the facilities and equipment necessary for safe and accurate compounding, including records of certification of facilities or equipment, if applicable.

- All equipment used to compound drug products is stored, used and maintained in accordance with manufacturers' specifications.

- All equipment used to compound drug products is calibrated before use to ensure accuracy.

- Documentation of each calibration is recorded in writing and kept in the pharmacy.

PHARMACY SECURITY

All pharmacists on duty are responsible for the security of the pharmacy, including effective control against theft and diversion. The space must be secured by a physical and/or electronic barrier that can be locked and, preferably, track entry into or out of the space. Pharmacy access by non-pharmacy personnel should be kept to a minimum, and any entry of non-pharmacy staff will be at the discretion of the pharmacist.

Only a pharmacist can have a key to the pharmacy. Other pharmacy staff, including interns, are not permitted to possess a key. One extra key may be kept by the pharmacy owner, building owner or manager in a tamper-evident container for the purpose of delivering the key to a pharmacist or providing access in case of an emergency.[33]

Security systems should include protection against outside and inside theft, including theft of electronic information and patient records. Pharmacies should install an alarm system, security cameras, "panic" buttons and adequate exterior lighting (and leave lights on after closing). There should be at least two employees on the premises during opening and closing. Staff members should be alert to suspicious activity and pay special attention to anyone who appears to be loitering, both inside and outside of the store.

If a robbery occurs, staff should remain calm and refrain from resisting, either verbally or physically. Robbers are often armed and are focused on getting what they came to take. Take notice of the appearance of the robber so a description can be provided to the police. Write down all observations, sound the alarm and call the police as soon as possible. Lock doors immediately to prevent re-entry. Protect the crime scene until the police arrive. Never try to apprehend or restrain the robber.

POLICIES AND PROCEDURES

Each pharmacy should have a Policy and Procedures (P&Ps) manual. A policy is a course of action for a specific activity, and the procedure (written into the policy) includes the steps that must be carried out by the staff. For example, the pharmacy's Quality Assurance P&Ps would outline the steps involved in conducting a quality assessment in order to reduce medication errors. P&Ps help keep the pharmacy running efficiently. The manual can protect the pharmacy in case of litigation and may be required for state or insurance reimbursement.

33 CCR 1714

Pharmacies must have P&Ps in place for:

- Action to be taken to protect the public when a licensed individual employed by or with the pharmacy is known to be <u>chemically, mentally or physically impaired</u> to the extent that it affects his or her ability to practice the profession or occupation authorized by his or her license.[34]

- Action to be taken to protect the public when a licensed individual employed by or with the pharmacy is known to have engaged in the <u>theft, diversion</u> or <u>self-use of prescription drugs belonging to the pharmacy</u>.[35]

- Operation of the pharmacy during the temporary absence of the pharmacist for breaks and meal periods, including authorized duties of personnel, the pharmacist's responsibilities for checking all work performed by ancillary staff and the pharmacist's responsibility for maintaining the security of the pharmacy.[36]

- Assuring confidentiality of medical information if the pharmacy maintains the required dispensing information for prescriptions, other than controlled substances, in a shared common electronic file.[37]

- The delivery of drugs and devices to a secure storage facility, if the pharmacy accepts deliveries when the pharmacy is closed, and there is no pharmacist present.[38]

- Compliance with the federal Combat Methamphetamine Epidemic Act of 2005.

- Reporting requirements to protect the public.[39]

- Establishing how a patient will receive a medication when a pharmacist has a conscientious objection to dispensing a drug.[40]

- Preventing the dispensing of a prescription when the pharmacist determines that the prescribed drug or device would cause a harmful drug interaction or would otherwise adversely affect the patient's medical condition.[41]

- Helping patients with limited or no English proficiency understand the information on the prescription container label in the patient's language, including the selected means to identify the patient's language and providing interpretive services in the patient's language.[42]

Hospital and compounding pharmacies have additional policies and procedures.[43, 44, 45]

RECORDKEEPING AND REPORTING REQUIREMENTS

Records for <u>drug acquisition</u> (e.g., invoices) and <u>disposition records</u> (e.g., prescription records, chart orders) are kept for at least <u>three years</u>. All schedule II drug records and inventories are kept separate from all others. <u>Pharmacies</u> are <u>responsible</u> for <u>maintaing records</u> and reporting to the board in compliance with legal requirements, as listed in the <u>tables on the following page</u>.

34   B&PC 4104(a), (c)
35   B&PC 4104(b), (c)
36   CCR 1714.1(f)
37   CCR 1717.1(e)
38   B&PC 4059.5(f)(1)
39   B&PC 4104
40   B&PC 733
41   B&PC 733
42   CCR 1707.5
43   CCR 70263
44   CCR 1735.5
45   B&PC 4074, CCR 1707.2(b)(3)

RECORD	MAINTAINED FOR AT LEAST
Hospital pharmacy chart orders for controlled substances	7 years
Patient acknowledgement of HIPAA	6 years
Transaction information, history and statement for most prescription drugs as required under the Drug Supply Chain Security Act	
Certificate of completion for continuing education	4 years
Community or clinic pharmacy prescriptions	3 years
Hospital pharmacy chart orders for non-controlled drugs	
Quarterly schedule II controlled substances inventory (state requirement)	
DEA Forms 222, CSOS records, power of attorney forms	
Purchase invoices for all prescription drugs	
Self-Assessment forms	
Documentation of the return of drugs to wholesaler or manufacturer	
Documentation of transfers or sales to other pharmacies, licensees and prescribers	
Theft and loss reports of controlled substances (DEA Forms 106)	
Biennial controlled substances inventory (all schedules; federal requirement)	2 years
Pseudoephedrine, ephedrine, phenylpropanolamine and norpseudoephedrine sales logs	
Patient medication profiles	1 year
Medication error/quality assurance reports	

ACTION/EVENT	REPORTING REQUIREMENTS
Change of pharmacist address or name	Within 30 days
Change of pharmacist-in-charge	Within 30 days
Changes in the pharmacy permit	Within 30 days
Theft by or impairment of a licensee	Within 14 days
Loss/theft of controlled drugs	Report to DEA immediately (one business day)
	Report to California Board of Pharmacy within 30 days
Bankruptcy, insolvency, receivership	Immediately

TASK	FREQUENCY
Completion of Self-Assessment form	Every odd-numbered year before July 1
	Within 30 days, when there is a new pharmacy permit, a change in PIC or a change in pharmacy location
Biennial controlled substances inventory (all schedules; federal requirement)	Every 2 years
Pharmacist continuing education (30 hours)	Every 2 years, except first cycle
Schedule II controlled substances inventory (state requirement)	Every 3 months
Medication error investigation	Within 2 days of error
Submitting dispensing data to CURES	Within 1 business day of dispensing any schedule II — V drug

PAPER PRESCRIPTION RECORDKEEPING SYSTEM FOR CONTROLLED SUBSTANCES

Pharmacies have <u>two options</u> for filing paper prescription records.

Paper Prescriptions Records Option 1 (Three Separate Files):

- A file for schedule II drugs dispensed.
- A file for schedules III, IV and V drugs dispensed.
- A file for all non-controlled drugs dispensed.

Paper Prescriptions Records Option 2 (Two Separate Files):

- A file for all schedule II drugs dispensed.
- A file for all other drugs dispensed (non-controlled and schedules III, IV and V drugs).

If option 2 is used, a prescription for a schedule III, IV or V drug must be made readily retrievable by use of a <u>red "C" stamp at least one inch high</u>. This enables a person to quickly flip through the records and pull them out from the rest. The red "C" is waived if the pharmacy has an electronic prescription recordkeeping system, which can identify controlled drugs by prescription number.

DEA CONTROLLED SUBSTANCES INVENTORY

Before opening a new pharmacy, there must be a complete inventory of all controlled substances. If there is no stock of controlled substances on hand, the record should show a zero inventory.

For regular inventories, the pharmacy needs to record the controlled substances currently on hand.

The federal requirement is to conduct an <u>inventory of all controlled substances</u> (schedules II – V) on a <u>biennial basis</u> (every two years).[46]

The California requirement is to conduct a <u>schedule II inventory</u> at least <u>every three months</u> (<u>quarterly</u>). In addition to the quarterly inventory, a <u>new PIC</u> must complete an inventory <u>within 30 days</u> of their appointment. It is recommended that the outgoing PIC also conduct an inventory. The inventory requires:

- A <u>physical count</u>, not an estimate, of all schedule II controlled substances. The biennial federal inventory can count as one of the state inventories for the year in which it was taken.
- A review of all acquisitions and dispositions. This means that all schedule II drugs that came into the pharmacy (i.e., from wholesaler deliveries) and all that went out (e.g., prescriptions, sales to other pharmacies/clinics) should be compared to see if the current inventory count corresponds correctly. If not, the cause of any discrepancies should be identified.[47]

Pharmacies must maintain inventory records at each location. Hospital pharmacies must conduct an inventory within the pharmacy and complete a separate report for each satellite location.

---

46 21 CFR 1304.11
47 CCR 1715.65

The <u>inventory records</u> of <u>schedule II drugs</u> must be kept <u>separate</u> from all other controlled substances. There is no requirement to submit a copy of the inventory to the DEA. If the pharmacist suspects a loss, the inventory is taken as soon as possible to confirm the loss. Losses and known causes must be reported to the board within <u>30 days of discovery</u> (when the loss was found) or within <u>14 days</u> if <u>theft, self-use</u> or <u>diversion by a board licensee</u> is the <u>cause</u>. If the cause is unknown, the pharmacy must <u>further investigate</u> to identify it and to take corrective action to prevent additional losses.

Inventory is counted at either the <u>beginning</u> or <u>close of business</u>. Inventory is <u>not performed during business hours</u> because it will change as medications are dispensed. The records must be in a written, typewritten or printed format. Inventory taken with a recording device must be reduced to writing promptly. The final form must be on paper and must contain:

- Date of the inventory and when it was taken (i.e., at the beginning or close of business)
- Names of controlled substances, dosage forms and strengths
- Number of dosage units or volume in each container (see comment below for how to count)
- Number of commercial containers (the type of container the drug came in from the supplier)

If a drug becomes scheduled or changes schedules, pharmacies must inventory <u>newly scheduled drugs on the date the scheduling became effective</u>.

When conducting an inventory of controlled substances, counting should be performed as follows:

- For sealed, <u>unopened</u> containers of all controlled substances, an <u>exact count</u> is needed. There is no need to open a sealed container; use the count listed on the manufacturer's drug container
- For <u>opened</u> containers of controlled substances:
  - All schedule <u>I and II</u> containers require an <u>exact count</u>
  - Schedule <u>III − V</u> containers that hold 1,000 dosage units or <u>less</u> can be <u>estimated</u>
  - Schedule <u>III − V</u> containers that hold <u>more</u> than 1,000 dosage units require an <u>exact count</u>

The inventory records must be kept (available for inspection) for <u>three years</u>.[48]

OFF-SITE STORAGE OF RECORDS

The board can grant waivers to allow off-site storage of records.[49] All records stored off-site must be kept in a <u>secure area</u> to prevent unauthorized access (e.g., at a records maintenance facility or at a commercial storage center). The waiver must be kept in the pharmacy. If the waiver for off-site storage of records is approved, a <u>signed copy</u> of the form will be returned to the pharmacy within <u>30 days</u>. Off-site storage of records is not allowed <u>until the board approves</u> the waiver. A new waiver is needed if the records are moved to a different location. The pharmacy must be able to produce the records within <u>two business days upon the request</u> of the board or another authorized officer of the law.[50, 51]

48 CCR 1718
49 CCR 1707
50 B&PC 4105
51 http://www.pharmacy.ca.gov/forms/offsite_storage.pdf (accessed 2020 Nov 13)

Prescription records are kept for <u>three years total</u>. Prescriptions for <u>non-controlled substances</u> must be kept <u>at the pharmacy</u> for at least <u>one year</u>. After that, the pharmacy can choose to store the prescriptions off-site for another two years. This is often done because there is not enough room in the pharmacy to keep all the paperwork. After three years have passed since the prescription was last dispensed, the pharmacy can throw the prescription away, although many pharmacies choose to keep prescriptions longer. Prescriptions for <u>controlled substances</u> must be kept <u>at the pharmacy</u> for at least <u>two years</u>. After that, the pharmacy can choose to store the prescriptions off-site for another year.

ORDER REQUIREMENTS FOR SUPPLYING AND BILLING DURABLE MEDICAL EQUIPMENT

Durable Medical Equipment (DME) is provided under Medicare Part B if the equipment was prescribed for use in the home. DME examples include:

- Blood glucose monitors, test strips, lancet devices and lancets
- Nebulizers and nebulized drugs
- Continuous Positive Airway Pressure (CPAP) machines
- Prosthetics, orthotics and supplies
- Ostomy supplies
- Walkers, scooters, canes and commode seats

Initially, the DME supplier, such as a pharmacy, receives a verbal or written dispensing order for the product the patient needs. Verbal or written dispensing orders can be used to provide the DME but cannot be used to bill Medicare. Billing requires a Detailed Written Order (DWO).

The DWO must include the prescriber's signature and date. It must contain the same information as a dispensing order with the addition of the date, signature and a detailed description of the item, such as the brand name and model number. Only supplies that are clearly related to the order can be added to the DWO by the supplier. Medicare does not accept PRN refills; refills must be detailed with the rest of the order.

The DWO must include:

- The item/s
- Dosage or concentration, if applicable
- Route of administration
- Frequency of use for test strips and lancets
- Duration of infusion, if applicable
- Quantity
- Number of refills

> **Example**
>
> MO is an 83-year-old female with Medicare. MO's physician's office calls her pharmacy and orders a glucose monitor with necessary supplies. The pharmacy fills and dispenses the order. The pharmacy can now create a DWO with the items provided (glucose monitor, test strips, lancets, calibration solution, battery, lancing device and lancets). This DWO is sent to the physician for their signature.
>
> The supplier is not permitted to add other items to the order that are not clearly related to the primary item ordered. MO's pharmacy must keep the original verbal dispensing order (written) and a copy of the completed DWO. When the pharmacy has both, the Centers for Medicare & Medicaid Services (CMS) can be billed for the DME.

DRUG PEDIGREES

There is an increasing prevalence of counterfeit, misbranded, adulterated and diverted prescription drugs in the United States. To prevent these drugs from entering the legitimate drug supply, the federal Drug Supply Chain Security Act (DSCSA) was passed in 2013. The DSCSA outlines steps to build a system to track and trace drugs as they are distributed within the United States.[52] This requirement applies to prescription drugs intended for human use. Many products are exempt, including: over-the-counter drugs, veterinary drugs, active pharmaceutical ingredients, blood products for transfusion, radioactive drugs, drugs used in imaging studies, certain intravenous products, certain medical gases (e.g., oxygen), homeopathic drugs and compounded preparations.

Manufacturers, wholesale distributors, pharmacies and repackagers (collectively referred to as "trading partners") are required to provide the subsequent purchaser with product tracing information when engaging in transactions involving certain prescription drugs. Anytime the drug is moved from one place to another, paperwork must follow.

Pharmacies must be able to capture and maintain transaction information (TI), transaction history (TH), and a transaction statement (TS), in paper or electronic form, for each drug product received for six years from the date of the transaction.[53] There are some situations that are exempt from this requirement, including dispensing drugs to a patient, providing drugs to a practitioner for office use, and distributing samples.

---

52 https://www.fda.gov/downloads/Drugs/GuidanceComplianceRegulatoryInformation/Guidances/UCM453225.pdf (accessed 2020 Nov 13)
53 http://www.pharmacy.ca.gov/publications/15_fall_script.pdf (accessed 2020 Nov 13)

TERM	DEFINITION
Transaction history	Statement including the transaction information for each prior transaction going back to the manufacturer of the product
Transaction information	Includes the: ■ Proprietary or established name or names of the product ■ Strength and dosage form of the product ■ National Drug Code (NDC) number of the product ■ Container size ■ Number of containers ■ Lot number of the product ■ Date of the transaction ■ Date of the shipment, if more than 24 hours after the date of the transaction ■ Business name and address of the person from whom ownership is being transferred ■ Business name and address of the person to whom ownership is being transferred
Transaction statement	Statement that the entity transferring ownership in a transaction: ■ Is authorized ■ Received the product from a person that is authorized ■ Received transaction information and a transaction statement from the prior owner of the product ■ Did not knowingly ship a suspect or illegitimate product ■ Had systems and processes in place to comply with verification requirements ■ Did not knowingly provide false transaction information ■ Did not knowingly alter the transaction history

DELIVERY OF DRUGS TO A PHARMACY

Drugs/devices are only delivered to the licensed premises and signed for and received by a <u>pharmacist</u>. Deliveries to a hospital pharmacy can be made to a <u>central receiving location</u> within the hospital. However, the drugs or devices must be delivered to the licensed pharmacy premises within <u>one working day</u> following the delivery, and the pharmacist on duty at that time must immediately <u>inventory</u> the drugs or devices.

A pharmacy can take delivery of drugs/devices when the pharmacy is closed, and no pharmacist is on duty, if all of the following requirements are met:[54]

■ The drugs/devices are placed in a secure storage facility in the same building as the pharmacy.

■ Only the PIC or a pharmacist designated by the PIC can access the secure storage facility after the drugs/devices have been delivered.

■ The secure storage facility has a means of indicating whether it has been entered after the drugs/devices have been delivered.

- The pharmacy keeps written P&Ps for the delivery of drugs/devices to a secure storage facility.
- The agent delivering drugs/devices leaves documents indicating the name and amount of each drug/device delivered.
- The pharmacy is responsible for the drugs/devices and keeping records relating to the delivery of the drugs/devices.

DRUG STOCK

Drugs that are adulterated, misbranded or expired cannot be purchased, traded, sold or transferred. Adulteration involves the drug itself (the quality), and misbranding involves incorrect or missing information on the label. The drug stock must be kept clean, orderly, properly stored, properly labeled and in-date (i.e., not expired).

ADULTERATION AND MISBRANDING

ADULTERATION VS. MISBRANDING

ADULTERATION (DRUG)	MISBRANDING (LABELING)
Filthy, putrid or decomposed	Lack of required information on the package and in the labeling or information is illegible (cannot be read)
Prepared or stored in unsanitary conditions	False or misleading information, imitating another drug or promising false cures
Contaminated	Special precautions needed to prevent decomposition not listed (e.g., protect from light)
Lack of quality controls or purity testing	Improper packaging, such as lack of Poison Prevention Packaging or incomplete labeling of additives
Drug is recognized in official compendia, but its strength is different from official standards, or the purity or quality is lower than the official standards	Packaging does not contain the proprietary (branded) or established common name, manufacturer or distributor and business location
Drug is not recognized in official compendia, but its strength is different from that listed on the label, or the purity or quality is lower than that listed on the label	Ingredients differ from the standard of strength, quality or purity, as determined by the test laid in the USP monograph
Examples: A vaccine which must be stored in the freezer has been stored in the refrigerator for the past week; vials of injectable pain medication are found to contain glass shards; a manufacturer does not perform adequate sterility tests before distributing an IV drug	**Examples:** An herbal product claims that it cures cancer; a product's labeling does not include information about risk in pregnancy; an oral contraceptive product is dispensed without the required patient package insert

Note that a medication can be both adulterated and misbranded. For example, a bottle of levothyoxine tablets are labeled as containing 100 mcg, but actually contain 50 mcg as determined by USP testing standards. The strength is lower than the standard (adulterated), and the product is falsely labeled (misbranded).

MONTHLY INSPECTION OF DRUG SUPPLY

The hospital drug supply must be inspected by a pharmacist, intern or technician at least every 30 days.[55] This includes automated dispensing systems, refrigerator, freezer and emergency supply stock. The inspection should include removing outdated, unusable (adulterated), recalled and mislabeled (misbranded) drugs. Look-alike, sound-alike drugs should not be stored close to each other. Records of inspections must be kept for at least three years. Irregularities must be reported within 24 hours to the PIC and the director or chief executive officer of the healthcare facility.

DRUG AND VACCINE SHORTAGES

Information regarding drug and vaccine shortages are available at the following websites:

- Drugs and vaccines
  - ❑ American Society of Health-System Pharmacists: *www.ashp.org/drugshortages*
  - ❑ Food and Drug Administration: *www.fda.gov/drugs/drugsafety/drugshortages/*
- Vaccines only
  - ❑ Centers for Disease Control and Prevention: *www.cdc.gov/vaccines/vac-gen/shortages/*

DRUG STORAGE

All drug stock needs to be kept in a secure manner and in proper storage conditions with the right temperature, humidity and light to keep it from becoming adulterated. The table below lists drugs that have additional storage requirements. Most of these drugs must be kept separated from the general drug stock to avoid misbranding and adulteration.

DRUG	STORAGE
Controlled Drugs	Locked cabinet or dispersed throughout the other drug stock (on the shelves)
Investigational New Drugs	Separate from other drug stock
Repackaged or Resold Drugs	Separate from other drug stock, assigned a Beyond-Use Date (BUD)
Recalled Drugs	Separate from other drug stock
Expired Drugs	Separate from other drug stock
Drug Samples	Separate from other drug stock; not allowed in retail pharmacies

DRUG SUPPLY AT NURSING STATIONS

Supplies of drugs for use in medical emergencies must be immediately available at each nursing unit or service area within an inpatient facility.[56] The emergency drug supply must be stored in a clearly marked portable container (e.g., a crash cart) which is sealed by the pharmacist in such a manner that a seal must be broken to gain access to the drugs. The contents of the container must be listed on the outside cover and must include the earliest expiration date of any drugs within.

---

55   22 CCR 70263(f), B&PC 4119.7(c), B&PC 4115(i)(3)
56   22 CCR 70263(f)

DRUG RECALLS

A drug recall occurs when a drug is removed from the market because it is defective or potentially harmful. Pharmacies must be positioned to receive notification of drug recalls. Federal, state or local law enforcement can request that a recall is carried out, but ultimately <u>recalls</u> are <u>issued</u> by either the <u>FDA</u> or the <u>drug manufacturer</u>. If the recall involves specific batches or lot numbers, the pharmacist will need to check the stock and remove the recalled drug. If there are multiple areas where a drug is stored within a facility, it is imperative that the drug is <u>removed from all storage areas</u>, including <u>patient care areas</u> and automated dispensing cabinets.

The FDA does not mandate that the pharmacy contact the patient. In a <u>Class I</u> recall, the <u>pharmacist</u> is <u>responsible</u> for determining which patients received the drug and <u>notifying</u> each <u>patient's prescriber</u>. The prescriber must decide whether to inform the patient.

The <u>manufacturer</u> of the recalled drug is <u>responsible for notifying</u> its customers; this includes <u>distributors and patients</u>. When a recalled drug is returned to the pharmacy, it is <u>quarantined</u> (separated) from other drugs prior to being returned or destroyed. Drugs that are quarantined for any reason (recalls, adulteration, expiration) must be labeled appropriately and placed in separate containers. Otherwise, they may be accidentally sent out to patients.

DRUG RECALL CLASSIFICATIONS

Drug recalls are classified based on the level of severity.

Class I: There is a reasonable probability that use of or exposure to the drug will cause serious adverse health consequences or death. Example: two lots of fentanyl transdermal 12 mcg/hour patches were recalled because some packages contained fentanyl 50 mcg/hour patches.

Class II: Use of or exposure to the drug can cause temporary or reversible adverse health consequences, or the probability of harm is remote. Example: several lots each of metformin extended-release, ranitidine and losartan were recalled due to containing unacceptable levels of a probable carcinogen, N-nitrosodimethylamine (NDMA).

Class III: Use of or exposure to the drug is not likely to cause adverse health consequences. Example: one lot of paliperidone extended-release 3 mg tablets was recalled due to failing dissolution tests.

A <u>pharmacy</u> or <u>outsourcing facility</u> must contact the recipient pharmacy, prescriber or patient and the board of pharmacy regarding a <u>compounded drug product</u> that is being recalled if both of the following apply:[57, 58, 59]

- Use of or exposure to the recalled compounded preparation can cause <u>serious adverse effects</u> or <u>death</u>.
- The recalled compounded preparation was dispensed or is intended for use in <u>California</u>.

Notice must be provided to the recipient pharmacy, prescriber or patient within <u>12 hours</u> of issuing the recall. The pharmacy or outsourcing facility must notify the board of pharmacy within <u>24 hours</u>.

57 B&PC 4126.9
58 B&PC 4127.8
59 B&PC 4129.9

A recall notice for a compounded drug preparation must be made as follows:

- If the recalled drug was dispensed directly to the patient, the notice must be made to the patient.

- If the recalled drug was dispensed directly to the prescriber, the notice must be made to the prescriber, who must ensure the patient is notified.

- If the recalled drug was dispensed directly to a pharmacy, the notice must be made to the pharmacy, who must notify the prescriber or patient, as appropriate. If the pharmacy notifies the prescriber, the prescriber must ensure the patient is notified.

If the <u>pharmacy</u> is made aware that a patient has been harmed by using a compounded product prepared by the pharmacy, the pharmacy must report the event to the <u>FDA *MedWatch*</u> program within <u>72 hours</u>. If the <u>outsourcing facility</u> is made aware that a patient has been harmed by using a compounded product prepared by the facility, the facility must report the event to the FDA *MedWatch* program within <u>15 calendar days</u>.[60]

RETURN, DISPOSAL OR REUSE OF DRUGS

PHARMACIES DONATING DRUGS FOR REDISTRIBUTION

California permits <u>drugs</u> in <u>single-use</u> or <u>sealed</u> packages from skilled nursing facilities, home healthcare and mail-order pharmacies to be <u>donated</u> to a repository and distribution program to help lower drug costs for low-income patients.[61] The requirements include:[62]

- Drugs must be <u>unused</u> and <u>not</u> expired. <u>No controlled substances</u> can be accepted as donations.

- Drugs are in unopened, tamper-evident packaging or unit-dose containers with lot numbers and expiration dates. Drugs have not been adulterated or misbranded.

- Drugs that require refrigeration must have been kept refrigerated.

- Drugs were received from a manufacturer or wholesaler (i.e., not from the public) or drugs were returned from a healthcare facility to which the drugs were originally issued.

Pharmacies can operate a drug repository and distribution program. Pharmacies that exist solely to operate the repository and distribution program can repackage donated drugs.[63]

PATIENTS RETURNING OR DISPOSING OF DRUGS

Pharmacies can accept returned prescription drugs from patients in certain situations (e.g., the wrong drug was dispensed). The returned drug <u>cannot</u> be <u>returned to stock/dispensed</u> to another patient. The pharmacy must <u>dispose</u> of the returned drug.

---

60 21 CFR 310.305(c)(1)(i)
61 H&SC 150202.5
62 H&SC 150204
63 H&SC 150204(i)(2)

It is important to dispose of drugs properly to <u>avoid drug abuse, accidental ingestion and environmental pollution</u>. The board has adopted the DEA regulations on drug take-back services.[64] There are a variety of safe and responsible ways to dispose of drugs through <u>take-back events, collection bin/receptacles</u> and <u>mail-back packages</u>. Most drugs should not be flushed down the toilet. Due to the high potential for misuse or abuse, the danger they pose with ingestion of a single dose, or both, a small number of medications should be flushed when no longer needed. See the Study Tip below for medications included in the FDA's Flush List.[65]

THE FDA'S FLUSH LIST

Drugs on the FDA's Flush List should be disposed of by flushing down the toilet. Select drugs on the list include:

- Buprenorphine
- Diazepam rectal gel
- Fentanyl-containing products
- Hydrocodone-containing products
- Hydromorphone
- Methadone
- Methylphenidate transdermal system (*Daytrana* patch)
- Morphine
- Oxycodone-containing products
- Oxymorphone
- Tapentadol

Pharmacy Take-Back Program

Pharmacies can voluntarily <u>register with the DEA</u> to <u>take back</u> unwanted drugs from patients by installing a <u>collection bin</u>. The bin must have a strong waterproof, removable liner. The container must have a rigid design and be kept securely locked. The patient or caregiver places the drugs into the collection bin themselves; the pharmacy staff should not know what has been placed into the bin. Drugs that have been placed in the bin cannot be removed by anyone in the pharmacy. Only the <u>reverse distributor</u> staff <u>is able to remove</u> the liner that contains the drugs. Two pharmacy staff must <u>watch</u> the removal and sign that they witnessed the disposal. Controlled substances can be <u>commingled</u> (mixed together) in the collection bin with <u>non-controlled drugs</u>. <u>Sharps and needles</u> (e.g., insulin syringes) and <u>illicit drugs</u> cannot be placed in the bin. Pharmacies cannot use the collection bins to dispose of their own <u>expired</u> or <u>recalled</u> drugs. The <u>following notifications</u> must be made to the board:

NOTIFICATION TO THE BOARD	TIMEFRAME
Establishment of drug take-back service	Within 30 days
Discontinuation of drug take-back service	Within 30 days
Any tampering with a collection bin	Within 14 days
Theft of deposited drugs	Within 14 days
Any tampering, damage or theft of a removed liner	Within 14 days
Disclosure of service and location of each receptacle	Annually, at time of facility license renewal

---

64 | CCR 1776
65 | https://www.fda.gov/drugs/disposal-unused-medicines-what-you-should-know/drug-disposal-fdas-flush-list-certain-medicines#FlushList (accessed 2020 Nov 13)

Pharmacies can also provide <u>pre-paid, pre-addressed</u> mailing envelopes for patients to return drugs to an authorized destruction location.[66] The patient puts the medications into the envelope and drops off the package at the post office. The package has a <u>plain wrapper</u>, without any markings or information that indicates what is inside. The package is <u>waterproof, spill-proof, tamper-evident, tear-resistant and sealable</u>. The package has a unique identification number that enables the package to be tracked.

Don't Rush to Flush

The California Board of Pharmacy has a campaign to avoid water pollution and reduce risk called *Don't Rush to Flush*. Patients should be instructed to safely dispose of <u>prescription, OTC</u> and <u>veterinary</u> medications by following the instructions below, and depositing into designated drug disposal bins.[67] There are now disposal bins in many locations, which can be found with a simple online search. Below are the patient instructions found on the *Don't Rush to Flush* website:

The Three Easy Steps for Patients to Safely Dispose of Unwanted Drugs

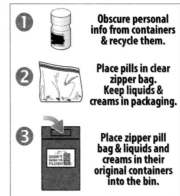

1. At home, remove pills and other solid medications from their containers and consolidate in a clear plastic zipper bag. Keep liquid and cream medication tightly sealed in their original containers. (Note – keep medications in their child-proof container until just prior to drop off.)

2. Remove, mark out, or otherwise obscure personal information from solid and liquid/cream medication containers to protect your personal information. Recycle containers for solid medications in your household recycling.

3. Bring zipper bag and any liquids/creams to a *Don't Rush to Flush* location and place in the bin – It's that easy!

1 Obscure personal info from containers & recycle them.

2 Place pills in clear zipper bag. Keep liquids & creams in packaging.

3 Place zipper pill bag & liquids and creams in their original containers into the bin.

Source: https://www.dontrushtoflush.org

MANDATORY REPORTING OF ABUSE AND NEGLECT

Each person licensed by the board (pharmacists, intern pharmacists and technicians) are "mandated reporters" of child abuse, elder abuse and neglect. Pharmacy staff have regular contact with vulnerable people, including children and elders. A report should be made when there is a reason to believe that a child/elder is a victim of abuse or neglect. The mandated reporters must phone law enforcement or protective services as soon as they can, and prepare and send a written report within <u>two working days</u> or <u>36 hours</u> of receiving the information concerning the incident. Failure to do so is a misdemeanor, punishable by up to six months in a county jail and/or a fine of $1,000.

---

66   CCR 1776.2
67   Locate drug disposal bins at www.dontrushtoflush.org (accessed 2020 Nov 13)

PHARMACY PRACTICE PART 1:
PRESCRIBING AND DISPENSING

CHAPTER CONTENTS

Healthcare Providers and Prescribing **30**
Self-Prescribing and Prescribing for Family Members.. 31
Prescriptions from Deceased Prescribers.. 31
Out-of-State and Foreign Prescribers 32
Requirements for a Valid Prescription.. **32**
Medication/Chart Orders 32
Transmission of an Outpatient Prescription... 33
Written Prescriptions for Medi-Cal Outpatient Drugs 34
Correcting Errors or Omissions 34
Converting a 30-Day Prescription to a 90-Day Prescription.. 35
Dispensing a 12-Month Supply of Hormonal Contraceptives.. 35
Prescription Refills... **36**
PRN Refills 36
Emergency Refills Without the Prescriber's Authorization.. 36
Refill Pharmacies 37
Prescription Transfers **37**
Labeling Requirements **38**
Expiration Dates 39
Format.. 39
Translation 40
Child-Resistant Packaging **40**
Written Patient Information **41**
Consumer Medication Information 41
Patient Package Inserts 41
Medication Guides 42
Risk Evaluation and Mitigation Strategy **43**
Dispensing and Counseling... **44**
Patient Medication Profiles 44
Drug Utilization Review 45
Patient Counseling 45
Notice to Consumers 48

Health Insurance Portability and Accountability Act 48

   The Notice of Privacy Practices 50

Drug Substitution and Selection **51**

   Generic Substitution 51

   Substituting Drug Formulations 52

   Substituting Biologics..52

   Drug Formularies..53

   Therapeutic Interchange Protocol...53

Dispensing Under Special Circumstances **54**

   Refusal to Dispense Based on Religious, Moral or Ethical Beliefs................................54

   Internet Pharmacies 54

   Telepharmacy at Remote Sites 54

   Dispensing Epinephrine Auto-Injectors...55

   Dispensing Blood Clotting Products for Home Use 56

   Dispensing Drugs During a Federal, State or Local Emergency.....................................56

   Dispensing Aid-in-Dying Drugs 57

Automated Drug Delivery Systems...**58**

Repackaging **59**

   Repackaging Drugs in Anticipation of Receiving Prescriptions....................................59

   Centralized Hospital Packaging 60

   Repackaging Previously Dispensed Drugs into Blister Packs..61

Compounding **61**

   Section 503A – Traditional Compounding...61

   Section 503B – Outsourcing Facilities 62

   Handling Hazardous Drugs 64

   Nuclear Pharmacy 64

PHARMACY PRACTICE PART 1:
PRESCRIBING AND DISPENSING

HEALTHCARE PROVIDERS AND PRESCRIBING

Some healthcare providers can prescribe independently while other healthcare providers can only dependently prescribe under a physician-directed protocol.[68] Any prescriber that prescribes controlled substances <u>must be registered with the DEA</u> and obtain a unique DEA number. In California, all prescribers are limited to prescribing within their scope of practice. Pharmacists should not fill a prescription if the practitioner is not prescribing within his or her <u>scope of practice</u>.

HEALTHCARE PROVIDER	TYPE OF PRESCRIBING/FURNISHING AUTHORITY
Physician (MD/DO)	Independent authority ■ Non-controlled and schedule II – V drugs.
Dentist Podiatrist (DPM) Veterinarian (DVM)	Independent authority, limited to scope of practice ■ Non-controlled and schedule II – V drugs.
Optometrist (OD)	Independent authority, limited to scope of practice ■ Non-controlled and schedule II – IV (does not include schedule V) drugs. ■ Must be certified with the Board of Optometry to prescribe drugs. These optometrists will have a letter T at the end of their license number. ■ For codeine-containing or hydrocodone-containing products, can prescribe a max three-day supply.[69] ■ Can prescribe other drugs relevant to their practice: oral analgesics, OTC drugs, oral antibiotics, topical antibiotics/antivirals/anesthetics/lubricants/anti-inflammatories (NSAIDs and steroid eye drops)/antihistamines, diagnostic drops (e.g., atropine, other mydriatics to dilate the pupils) and glaucoma eye drops.[70]

68 H&SC 11150
69 B&PC 3041(b)
70 B&PC 3041(b)(14)

HEALTHCARE PROVIDER	TYPE OF PRESCRIBING/FURNISHING AUTHORITY
Naturopathic Doctors (ND)	Independent authority, limited to the following: ■ Epinephrine to treat anaphylaxis. ■ Natural and synthetic hormones (naturopathic doctor must have a DEA number to prescribe controlled substances, including testosterone).[71, 72] ■ Vitamins, minerals, amino acids, glutathione, botanicals and their extracts, homeopathic medicines, electrolytes, sugars and diluents, only when such substances are available without a prescription. A furnishing number is required for NDs to prescribe. It is typically the ND's license number preceded by the letters NDF. Dependent authority: ■ All other non-controlled and schedule III – V drugs (does not include schedule II).
Registered Pharmacist (RPh)	Independent authority, limited to the following: ■ Emergency contraception, self-administered hormonal contraception. ■ Travel medicine recommended by the CDC, not requiring a diagnosis. ■ Routine immunizations recommended by the CDC for patients ≥ 3 years old. ■ Naloxone. ■ Prescription nicotine replacement products. ■ Pre-exposure prophylaxis (PrEP), max 60 days every 2 years, future fills must be by PCP. ■ Post-exposure prophylaxis (PEP). Dependent authority: ■ All other non-controlled and schedule II – V drugs.
Certified Nurse Midwife (CNM) Nurse Practitioner (NP) Physician Assistant (PA)	Dependent authority ■ Non-controlled and schedule II – V drugs.

SELF-PRESCRIBING AND PRESCRIBING FOR FAMILY MEMBERS

In California, prescribers can self-prescribe non-controlled substances.[73] Prescribers can prescribe non-controlled and controlled substances to family members as long as there is a valid physician/patient relationship, a legitimate medical purpose and a good faith exam.[74]

PRESCRIPTIONS FROM DECEASED PRESCRIBERS

If a valid prescription was written when the prescriber was living, the prescription is considered valid until all refills are gone, and no more than six months from the date written for controlled substances and one year for non-controlled substances (standard of practice).[75, 76] The pharmacist should encourage the patient to look for a new doctor as soon as possible and not to wait until the prescription is expired or the refills are gone. If another doctor takes over the deceased prescriber's practice, the pharmacist should request a new prescription from this prescriber.

71   http://www.naturopathic.ca.gov/licensees/notice_hormone.shtml (accessed 2020 Nov 13)
72   http://www.pharmacy.ca.gov/publications/05_oct_script.pdf (accessed 2020 Nov 13)
73   H&SC 11170
74   http://www.pharmacy.ca.gov/publications/13_mar_script.pdf (accessed 2020 Nov 13)
75   H&SC 11166
76   http://www.pharmacy.ca.gov/publications/13_fall_script.pdf (accessed 2020 Nov 13)

OUT-OF-STATE AND FOREIGN PRESCRIBERS

A pharmacist <u>can dispense</u> a drug or device <u>pursuant to</u> a written or oral <u>order from a prescriber licensed in another state</u> if the out-of-state prescriber has a <u>license equivalent</u> to that required of a <u>California prescriber</u>.[77,78] The pharmacist may need to verify the prescriber's license and determine whether he or she is authorized to prescribe. The pharmacist can then dispense the prescription to the patient.

As a general rule, a pharmacist <u>cannot fill a prescription from another country</u>. The District of Columbia and the U.S. territories (which include Puerto Rico, the Virgin Islands, Guam and American Samoa) are treated the same as U.S. states for filling prescriptions. Refer to the Controlled Substances Part 3 chapter for information on scheduled drug prescriptions from out-of-state prescribers.

REQUIREMENTS FOR A VALID PRESCRIPTION

A prescription must have the following:[79]

- <u>Patient</u> name and address
- <u>Drug</u> name and quantity
- <u>Directions</u> for use
- <u>Date</u> of issue
- <u>Prescriber information</u> (rubber stamped, typed or printed by hand or typeset):
  - ❏ Name, business address and telephone number
  - ❏ License classification
  - ❏ DEA number, if a controlled substance is prescribed
- <u>Condition or purpose</u> of prescribed drug, <u>if requested by the patient</u>
- <u>Prescriber signature</u>

MEDICATION/CHART ORDERS

Medication orders, or chart orders, are the prescriber's orders for drugs and other items (such as labs and procedures) for institutionalized patients (i.e., patients in a hospital or long-term care facility). A medication order would include similar information to a prescription, such as the patient name, drug name, dose, frequency and prescriber's signature. A prescriber can handwrite an order in the patient's <u>physical paper chart</u> or enter it into the patient's <u>electronic medical record</u>.

Prescribers can also issue <u>face-to-face verbal</u> and <u>telephone</u> orders for hospital patients. Written orders are preferred over verbal orders to reduce medication errors. There could be an emergency situation, such as a code, where a drug must be administered immediately. In this situation, it would be appropriate for a prescriber to issue a verbal order and authenticate it at a later time.

77 http://www.pharmacy.ca.gov/publications/07_jul_script.pdf (accessed 2020 Nov 13)
78 CCR 1717(d)
79 B&PC 4040

For example, a nurse could report that a patient is experiencing nausea, and the prescriber could instruct the nurse to administer ondansetron. The nurse would enter the order, note the prescriber's name and sign the order. The prescriber has 48 hours to physically or electronically countersign the order.[80]

A copy of the chart order for non-controlled substances must be kept at the hospital for at least three years.[81] All orders for controlled substances in a hospital setting must be kept for a minimum of seven years.[82]

In addition to individual medication orders, drugs can be provided under a standing order, protocol or order set, which are treatment plans designed to help direct care for select conditions. The use of standing orders, order sets and protocols will be described in a facility's policies and procedures.

TRANSMISSION OF AN OUTPATIENT PRESCRIPTION

An employee or agent (e.g., a nurse or secretary), under the supervision of a prescriber, can transmit prescriptions for non-controlled and schedule III – V drugs to a pharmacist.[83] The pharmacist must document who is calling in or faxing the prescription on behalf of the prescriber.[84] The agent can also prepare a prescription for the prescriber to sign and date.

Orally transmitted prescriptions are received and reduced to writing by a pharmacist or intern pharmacist working under the direct supervision of a pharmacist.[85] "Reduce to writing" means to write the oral prescription information onto the pharmacy's prescription blank. If orally transmitted, the pharmacist who received the prescription is identified by initialing the prescription, and if dispensed by another pharmacist, the dispensing pharmacist also initials the prescription.

Faxed prescriptions can only be received from a prescriber's office (not from the patient).

A patient or the patient's agent can deposit a prescription into a secure container (a drop box) that is at the same address as the pharmacy. If a pharmacy chooses to use a drop box, the pharmacy is responsible for the security and confidentiality of the prescriptions placed into it.[86]

The name or initials of the dispensing pharmacist must be documented for each prescription. Commonly, the pharmacist will handwrite their initials on the pharmacy's duplicate copy of the prescription label or use a unique login for an electronic pharmacy workflow software which will electronically document who verified each prescription.[87, 88]

---

80 22 CCR 70263(g)
81 B&PC 4081, B&PC 4105, B&PC 4333
82 H&SC 11159
83 https://www.deadiversion.usdoj.gov/fed_regs/rules/2010/fr1006.htm (accessed 2020 Nov 13)
84 B&PC 4071
85 B&PC 4070
86 CCR 1713 (c)
87 CCR 1717(b)(1)
88 CCR 1712(a)

WRITTEN PRESCRIPTIONS FOR MEDI-CAL OUTPATIENT DRUGS

Since 2008, the Federal Centers for Medicare and Medicaid Services (CMS) has required the use of tamper-resistant pads for all Medi-Cal (California Medicaid program) outpatient prescriptions in order to be reimbursed by the government. The tamper-resistant forms must contain the three security features in the table below.

The California Board of Pharmacy requires certain security features on prescription forms used to prescribe controlled substances.[89] A California security form for controlled substances exceeds the Medi-Cal prescription requirements for outpatient drugs.[90] Therefore, a California security form can also be used to prescribe outpatient drugs for Medi-Cal beneficiaries. California security forms are discussed further in the Controlled Substances Part 3 chapter.

MEDI-CAL PRESCRIPTION FORM REQUIREMENTS

SECURITY FEATURES	EXAMPLES
Prevent unauthorized copying of a completed or blank prescription form	▪ The word "void" appears when this prescription is photocopied ▪ Forms with watermarks
Prevent the erasure or modification of information written on the prescription by the provider	▪ Quantity check-off boxes so that the prescriber can indicate the quantity by checking the applicable box ▪ Check boxes must be printed on the form so that the prescriber can indicate the number of refills ordered ▪ Preprinted text "Rx is void if more than ____ Rxs on paper" on prescription paper
Prevent the use of counterfeit prescription	▪ Each prescription form is serially numbered ▪ Certain text or images are printed in thermochromic ink ▪ Microprint signature line

CORRECTING ERRORS OR OMISSIONS

Errors or omissions on a prescription for non-controlled drugs can be revised by the pharmacist if it is minor (e.g., misspelling a drug name) or after consultation with the prescriber if it is significant. The pharmacist will need to document the discussion. Alternatively, after verification with the prescriber, the prescription can be re-written as an oral prescription and the original prescription will be voided. The prescriber can also resend another prescription via electronic transmission or fax.[91] See the Controlled Substances Part 3 chapter for information on correcting errors or omissions on controlled substance prescriptions.

89   H&SC 11164(a)
90   http://www.pharmacy.ca.gov/publications/17_jun_script.pdf (accessed 2020 Nov 13)
91   CCR 1761

CONVERTING A 30-DAY PRESCRIPTION TO A 90-DAY PRESCRIPTION

A patient may prefer to convert a prescription from a 30-day supply to a 90-day supply to minimize trips to the pharmacy or to save on prescription copays.

It is permissible to dispense up to a 90-day supply of a drug when the initial prescription specified a shorter time period (e.g., a 30-day supply) as long as the following requirements are met:[92]

- The prescription is not for a controlled substance or a psychiatric drug.
- The patient has completed an initial 30-day supply of the drug with no negative effects, or the patient previously received the same medication with a 90-day supply.
- The total quantity dispensed (including the refills) does not exceed the amount authorized on the prescription.
- The pharmacist notifies the prescriber of the larger quantity dispensed.

A pharmacist cannot dispense a greater supply of a drug if:

- The prescriber indicates, either orally or in writing, "No change to quantity," or other words of similar meaning.
- The prescriber indicates that dispensing the prescribed amount is medically necessary.

DISPENSING A 12-MONTH SUPPLY OF HORMONAL CONTRACEPTIVES

California has expanded patient access to hormonal contraceptives (birth control) by allowing patients to pick up an annual supply at one time. Hormonal contraceptives include the oral contraceptives, the patch (e.g., *Xulane*), the ring (e.g., *NuvaRing)* and the injection (e.g., *Depo-SubQ Provera)*. Health plans are required to provide coverage for up to a 12-month supply.[93] Dispensing an annual supply has many benefits, including increased adherence, which reduces unintended pregnancies. This decreases healthcare costs by reducing the number of pregnancy tests and pregnancies.[94]

At a patient's request and with a valid prescription, the pharmacy must dispense up to a 12-month supply of a hormonal contraceptive (all at one time).[95] For example, if a patient presents a prescription for *Sprintec* #28 tablets and 11 refills, the patient can request for the entire annual supply to be dispensed at once. The total quantity dispensed (including the refills) cannot exceed the amount authorized on the prescription. Using the same example as above, if the prescriber only authorized a prescription for *Sprintec* #28 tablets and 2 refills, then the pharmacist can only dispense a three-month supply. If the prescriber indicates that there cannot be any change to the quantity or if the prescriber indicates that dispensing the initial amount is medically necessary, the pharmacist must dispense the quantity the prescriber has specified. In the *Sprintec* example, that would mean a quantity of 28 tablets must be dispensed.

---

92   B&PC 4064.5 (a-e)
93   H&SC 1367.25(d)
94   SB-999
95   B&PC 4064.5(f)

PRESCRIPTION REFILLS

Refills of prescriptions are permitted as long as the refills were authorized orally, in writing or electronically by the prescriber.[96] Although there is no refill limit for non-scheduled drugs, refills should not be dispensed after one year from date of issue.

All scheduled drug prescriptions expire six months from the date of issue. There are no refill limits for schedule V drugs, but there are restrictions for schedule III and IV drugs (see the Controlled Substances Part 3 chapter).

Refills for Schedule II controlled substances are prohibited. See the Controlled Substances Part 3 chapter for further discussion.

PRN REFILLS

PRN (as-needed) refills are acceptable for non-controlled substances, according to California law. Since it is standard of practice that prescriptions for non-controlled substances expire one year from date of issue, PRN refills should not be refilled after one year from the date of issue.

If a prescriber writes for a non-scheduled drug for a 30-day supply per fill with "PRN refills," then it can be refilled 11 times before it expires. Notice that the amount of refills allowed depends on the days supply the prescription is written for. If it is written for a 90-day supply, then the pharmacist can dispense the original fill and three refills before the prescription expires. PRN refills for controlled substances are not acceptable.[97]

EMERGENCY REFILLS WITHOUT THE PRESCRIBER'S AUTHORIZATION

California allows emergency refills without the prescriber's authorization if the prescriber is unavailable to authorize the refill for non-controlled drugs and schedule III – V drugs. A pharmacist must use professional judgment to determine if failure to refill the prescription might interrupt the patient's ongoing care or if it would have a significant adverse effect on their well-being.[98] The pharmacist must have made a reasonable effort to contact the prescriber. The emergency refill must be properly documented and the prescriber must be notified of the emergency refill within a reasonable amount of time.

California does not specify a quantity limit for an emergency refill for non-controlled drugs, so the pharmacist must use his or her professional judgment when deciding to dispense a full or partial refill amount.[99] For schedule III – V drugs, the pharmacist can only provide a reasonable amount to cover the emergency period until the prescriber can be contacted for a refill authorization. For controlled substances, the pharmacist must document on the reverse side of the prescription the date and quantity of the refill, that the prescriber was not available and the reason for refilling without the prescriber's authorization.[100]

Pharmacists cannot dispense an emergency refill for schedule II drugs, but an emergency verbal order could potentially be obtained (see the Controlled Substances Part 3 chapter).

96   B&PC 4063
97   B&PC 4063
98   B&PC 4064, H&SC 11201
99   B&PC 4064(a)
100   H&SC 11201

REFILL PHARMACIES

Retail pharmacies can use central fill (or refill) pharmacies to fill new prescriptions and refills. If the two pharmacies use a common electronic file, policies and procedures must be in place to prevent unauthorized disclosures. The originating pharmacy and the refill pharmacy must have a <u>contract</u> outlining the refill arrangement, or the pharmacies must have the <u>same owner</u>. In addition to the normal requirements for a prescription label, the name and address of the refilling and/or the originating pharmacy must be included on the label. The patient must be provided with written information, either on the label or on the container that describes which pharmacy to contact for questions. Both pharmacies are responsible for the accuracy of the fills and both need to keep complete records of the fills. The <u>originating pharmacy</u> is responsible for <u>counseling patients, maintaining the medication profiles and performing a drug utilization review</u> before delivery of each prescription.

PRESCRIPTION TRANSFERS

Prescriptions can be transferred from one pharmacy to another. This must be done by direct communication between two <u>pharmacists</u> or <u>interns</u>.[101] <u>Non-controlled drugs</u> can be transferred <u>as many times as there are refills</u>. <u>Schedule III – V</u> drugs can only be <u>transferred once</u>, unless a shared database is used.

Information kept by each pharmacy must at least include:[102]

- Identification of the pharmacists or intern pharmacists involved in transferring information.
- Name and identification code (i.e., pharmacy store number) or address of the pharmacy from which the prescription was received or to which the prescription was transferred. Each pharmacy receives the other pharmacy's information.
- Original date and last dispensing date.
- Number of refills and date originally authorized.
- Number of refills transferred (remaining refills that have not been dispensed).

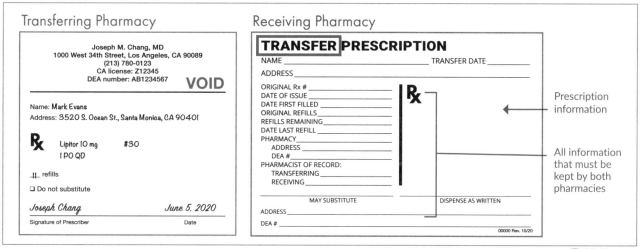

©RxPrep, Inc.

101   CCR 1717(e)
102   https://cdn.ymaws.com/www.ascp.com/resource/resmgr/files/DEA_Redirection_Issue.pdf (accessed 2020 Nov 13)

Schedule II prescriptions <u>cannot be transferred</u>; written prescriptions should be returned to the patient for filling elsewhere. If a schedule II prescription was sent electronically and has not been filled, the electronic prescription can be forwarded to another pharmacy to fill. This is not considered a transfer. See the Controlled Substances Part 3 chapter for further discussion on transferring controlled substance prescriptions.

LABELING REQUIREMENTS

Prescription containers must have all of the following information:[103]

REQUIREMENTS FOR PRESCRIPTION LABELS

1. Patient name
2. Drug name, strength, quantity
3. Directions for use
4. Purpose of the drug (if written on the prescription)
5. Prescriber name
6. Physical description of the drug (including color, shape and imprint)
7. Expiration date
8. Name and address of dispenser
9. Serial or prescription number
10. Date of issue

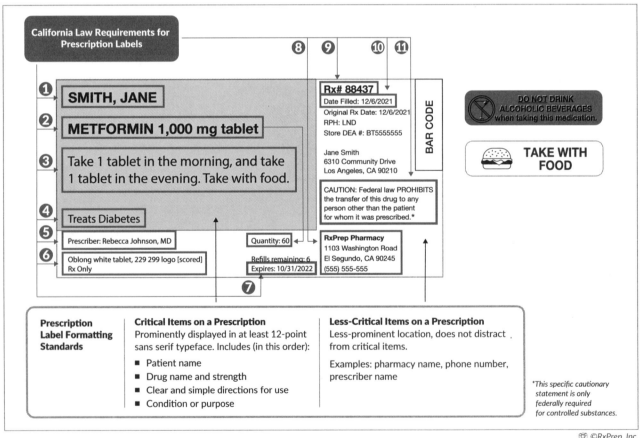

When a <u>brand name</u> drug is dispensed, the brand name should be listed on the prescription label (e.g., *Roxicodone*). The manufacturer name is not required because the brand name can be used to identify the manufacturer.

When a <u>generic</u> drug is dispensed, the label must include the <u>generic name</u>, the statement "<u>generic for</u> [insert brand name equivalent]" to indicate the <u>brand name drug equivalent</u> to the dispensed generic drug, and the <u>generic drug manufacturer</u> (e.g., oxycodone, generic for *Roxicodone*, MFR: *Actavis*). There are often multiple manufacturers of the same generic drug (e.g., generic oxycodone is manufactured by *Actavis, Amneal, Sun* and others).

EXPIRATION DATES

The expiration date on the prescription label can be either the <u>manufacturer's</u> expiration date or <u>one year from the date the drug is dispensed</u>, whichever is earlier.[104] The expiration date will usually be notated with a <u>month and year</u>, and the drug is acceptable to use until the <u>end of the month</u> in which it expires. For example, if the expiration date is 3/2022, then the expiration date is March 31, 2022. The monographs for some preparations state how the labeled expiration date must be determined. For example, the labeling for *Augmentin* states that the beyond-use date (BUD) after reconstitution is ten days. If a drug container <u>does not have an expiration date</u>, it is considered <u>misbranded</u>, is treated as an expired drug and should not be dispensed.

FORMAT

There are formatting standards for multiple unit prescription labels in order to promote patient understanding of the medication use, increase adherence and reduce medication errors. The content of the prescription label is often the only drug information the patient will read. It must be easy to understand and include the proper auxiliary labels. These standards do not apply to inpatient medications since those are labeled for a healthcare professional to administer.

Each of the following items must be compiled in one area of the label that comprises at least <u>50% of the label</u>. Each item must be printed in at least a <u>12-point sans serif typeface</u>, and listed in the following order:[105]

- <u>Patient name</u>
- <u>Drug name</u> (trade/brand name or generic + "generic for _____" + manufacturer) and <u>strength</u>
  - ❑ If the brand is not widely used, it can be left off
- <u>Directions for use</u>
- <u>Condition or purpose</u> for which the drug was prescribed if this was on the prescription

For added emphasis, the label must also <u>highlight</u> in <u>bold</u> typeface or <u>color</u>, or use <u>blank space</u> to set off the 4 critical items above. Less critical information should be placed away from the items above (e.g., at the bottom of the label or in another less prominent location) to avoid distracting from the key information. These additional elements may appear in any style, font and size typeface (see label image on previous page).

104 http://www.pharmacy.ca.gov/publications/02_jan_script.pdf (accessed 2020 Nov 13)
105 CCR 1707.5

Directions for use should be clear and easy to interpret. Time periods should be specified and numbers should be used instead of words when appropriate. For example, instead of "Take two tablets twice daily" the label should read "Take 2 tablets in the morning and 2 tablets in the evening." Avoid hourly intervals (such as "every 8 hours") since this requires the patient to count. In general, specifying an exact time should be avoided unless the drug must be taken at exact times (e.g., tacrolimus for a transplant patient, with times specified on the prescription, 12 hours apart). Specifying an exact time can be too restrictive for patients who are busy with work, school or other responsibilities. Jargon or Latin terminology should not be used.

TRANSLATION

At the request of a patient or patient's representative, the pharmacist must provide translated directions for use, which must be printed on the prescription container, label or on a supplemental document. If translated directions for use appear on a prescription container or label, the English language version of the directions also need to appear on the container or label, whenever possible, and can appear on other areas of the label outside of the patient centered area. When it is not possible for the English language directions for use to appear on the container or label, it should be provided on a supplemental document. A pharmacist can use translations made available by the board. A pharmacist is not required to provide translated directions for use beyond the languages that the board has made available in translated form.[106,107]

CHILD-RESISTANT PACKAGING

Before the implementation of the Poison Prevention Packaging Act (PPPA) in 1970, accidental poisoning was the leading cause of injury in young children. At that time, there was no standard way to protect children from ingesting common dangerous substances, including drugs and household cleaners. The PPPA required the use of child-resistant (C-R) containers for many OTC products, most oral prescription drugs and dangerous household chemicals. C-R containers are designed to prevent at least 85% of children from opening the container without a demonstration and prevent at least 80% of children from opening following a demonstration. At least 90% of adults should be able to open the container.

The PPPA mandates that a new plastic container and closure (e.g., bottle and plastic cap) must be used for each prescription dispensed. This requirement is meant to avoid damage to the seal from "wear and tear," which can reduce the C-R effectiveness. If a glass container is used, only the top closure needs to be replaced. Reversible containers (C-R when turning the closure one direction, but not child-resistant in the other direction) are permitted if dispensed in the C-R mode, but are not recommended.

EXEMPTIONS TO C-R PACKAGING

- **Sublingual nitroglycerin**
- **Oral contraceptives**
- **Hormone replacement therapy**
- Powdered unflavored aspirin
- Effervescent aspirin
- Powdered iron preparations
- Effervescent acetaminophen

106   http://www.pharmacy.ca.gov/publications/translations.shtml (accessed 2020 Nov 13)
107   B&PC 4076.6

The patient or prescriber can request "easy-open," non-C-R containers. The prescriber can waive the use of a C-R container for a single prescription. The patient can provide a blanket waiver for all prescriptions. The pharmacist must document the waiver request with the patient's signature.

C-R packaging is not required for drugs administered by a healthcare provider. For the people who might have difficulty opening C-R containers, the PPPA allows manufacturers to package one size of OTC drugs in a non-C-R (easy-open) container as long as the same product is also available in a C-R container. The package must have the warning, "This package is for households without young children" or "Package Not Child-Resistant."

WRITTEN PATIENT INFORMATION

There are four types of written information that can be provided to the patient:

- Consumer Medication Information (CMI) leaflets
- Patient Package Inserts (PPIs)
- Medication Guides (MedGuides)
- Instructions for Use

CONSUMER MEDICATION INFORMATION

The FDA mandates that useful written patient information be provided to patients with each new prescription. CMI handouts are the paper leaflets of drug information that are put inside the prescription bag or stapled to the outside. These are not reviewed or approved by the FDA.

- The information should be simplified for patients to understand and should reflect the FDA-approved package insert.
- They should explain how to use the drug, receive benefit and avoid harm.

PATIENT PACKAGE INSERTS

In the 1970s, the FDA required that all oral contraceptives be dispensed with the FDA-approved patient package insert (PPI) in order for the patient to be fully informed of the benefits and risks involved with the use of these drugs. Oral contraceptives for birth control were first available in 1960 and, after five years, 6.5 million women were using "the pill." Initially, the estrogen content was much higher than the pills in use today. Consequently, there was a higher incidence of clotting. The FDA required the PPIs due to the lack of awareness of safety risks.

For oral contraceptives, the PPI must be given each time the drug is dispensed in the outpatient or retail setting, with both the initial fill and with refills. In an institutional setting such as a hospital or long-term care facility, the PPI must be provided to the patient prior to the administration of the first dose and every 30 days thereafter.[108] If the PPI is not provided as required by law, it is considered misbranding.

Other drugs can voluntarily come with an FDA-approved PPI if the manufacturer feels that there is important information that the patient should know about the drug.

108   21 CFR 310.515

MEDICATION GUIDES

MedGuides are FDA-approved patient handouts for many prescription medicines that may have a serious and significant health concern.

The FDA requires that MedGuides be issued with drugs or biologics that require patient education about how to prevent serious side effects, the risks of side effects (to guide decision-making) or if adherence to specific instructions is essential to effectiveness. The manufacturer must supply the MedGuides to the dispenser by providing the physical handouts or the electronic file so the pharmacy can print them out for the patient.

There are over 300 medications that require MedGuides. The full list can be found on the FDA website.[109] Select drugs that require MedGuides can be found in the table below.

The MedGuide must be given when:

- A drug is dispensed in the outpatient setting for patient self-administration without the supervision of a healthcare provider (initial fill and refills).
- The first time the drug is dispensed to a healthcare provider for administration to a patient in an outpatient setting.
- The patient or their caregiver asks for it.
- The MedGuide has been revised.
- The drug is subject to a REMS that requires a MedGuide.

SELECT DRUGS WITH MEDGUIDES, EXAMPLES OF COMMON DRUGS IN CLASS

Antidepressants	NSAIDS
Bupropion (Wellbutrin)	Celecoxib (Celebrex)
Citalopram (Celexa)	Diclofenac (Voltaren, Flector, Cambia)
Doxepin (Sinequan)	Diclofenac/Misoprostol (Arthrotec)
Duloxetine (Cymbalta)	Etodolac
Escitalopram (Lexapro)	Ibuprofen (Advil, Motrin)
Fluoxetine (Prozac)	Ibuprofen/Hydrocodone (Vicoprofen)
Imipramine	Indomethacin (Indocin)
Mirtazapine (Remeron)	Ketorolac (SPRIX)
Nortriptyline (Pamelor)	Meloxicam (Mobic)
Paroxetine (Paxil)	Nabumetone
Sertraline (Zoloft)	Naproxen (Aleve, Naprosyn, Anaprox)
Trazodone (Desyrel)	Oxaprozin (Daypro)
Venlafaxine (Effexor)	
Insomnia Drugs	**Long-Acting Beta-Agonists**
Eszopiclone (Lunesta)	Arformoterol (Brovana)
Ramelteon (Rozerem)	Formoterol (Foradil Aerolizer, Perforomist)
Temazepam (Restoril)	Formoterol/Budesonide (Symbicort)
Triazolam (Halcion)	Salmeterol (Serevent Diskus)
Zaleplon (Sonata)	Salmeterol/Fluticasone (Advair Diskus, Advair HFA)
Zolpidem (Ambien)	

---

109   https://www.fda.gov/drugs/drug-safety-and-availability/medication-guides (accessed 2020 Nov 13)

SELECT DRUGS WITH MEDGUIDES, EXAMPLES OF COMMON DRUGS IN CLASS

ADHD Drugs	**Diabetes Drugs**
Atomoxetine (*Strattera*)	Exenatide (*Bydureon, Byetta*)
Dexmethylphenidate (*Focalin*)	Pioglitazone (*Actos*)
Dextroamphetamine (*Dexedrine*)	Pioglitazone/Metformin (*Actoplus Met*)
Dextroamphetamine/Amphetamine (*Adderall*)	Rosiglitazone (*Avandia*)
Lisdexamfetamine (*Vyvanse*)	Rosiglitazone/Metformin (*Avandamet*)
Methylphenidate (*Concerta, Daytrana, Metadate CD, Methylin, Ritalin*)	Canagliflozin (*Invokana*), empagliflozin (*Jardiance*), others
Antipsychotics	**Antiarrhythmics**
Aripiprazole (*Abilify*)	Amiodarone (*Cordarone, Pacerone*)
Olanzapine (*Relprevv* Injection)	
Quetiapine (*Seroquel*)	
Retinoids	**Others**
Acitretin (*Soriatane*)	Anticoagulants
Isotretinoin (*Absorica, Amnesteem, Claravis, Myorisan, Zenatane*)	Alendronate and other bisphosphonates
	Many monoclonal antibodies
	Quinolone antibiotics
	Etanercept (*Enbrel*)
	Erythropoeitin stimulating agents
	Fentanyl (*Duragesic, Fentora*)
	Pimecrolimus (*Elidel*)
	Raloxifene (*Evista*)
	Tacrolimus (*Protopic, Prograf, Astagraf*)
	Tamoxifen (*Soltamox*)
	Teriparatide (*Forteo*)
	Testosterone (*Androgel*)
	Varenicline (*Chantix*)

RISK EVALUATION AND MITIGATION STRATEGY

The FDA Amendments Act of 2007 gave the FDA the authority to require a REMS from manufacturers to ensure that the benefits of certain drugs and biologics outweigh the risks. If the FDA feels that the drug has serious safety concerns that would not be sufficiently addressed with the use of boxed warnings and MedGuides, they can mandate the use of a REMS. This ensures that the risks are known and are managed adequately.

The manufacturer, also known as the drug's sponsor, develops the REMS and gets FDA-approval before implementation. It can be required for a new drug or drug class, or when safety issues arise with an existing drug. There are four parts to a REMS:

1. Communication plans
2. Elements to assure safe use
3. Implementation systems
4. MedGuides

DRUG	RISK	REMS
Thalidomide	Severe birth defects	*Thalomid* REMS Program (previously called the STEPS Program)[110] Negative pregnancy test required prior to dispensing each prescription
Isotretinoin	Severe birth defects	iPledge Program[111] Two negative pregnancy tests required before first fill & one negative test prior to dispensing each subsequent prescription
Clozapine	Neutropenia	Clozapine REMS program Monitor the absolute neutrophil count (ANC)
Phentermine/Topiramate (Qsymia)	Severe birth defects	*Qsymia* REMS Program[112] MedGuide required, healthcare training program, dispensed only through certified pharmacies
Opioid analgesics	High abuse potential, life-threatening respiratory depression	Educate providers about treating and monitoring pain by completing REMS-compliant training and taking knowledge assessments. Dispense with MedGuide as required. MedGuide requirements are product specific (i.e., not all opioids require a MedGuide). Educate prescriber and patient on safe use, risks, storage and disposal.
Flibanserin (Addyi)	Risk of hypotension and syncope due to an interaction with alcohol	*Addyi* REMS Program No alcohol use while taking *Addyi*, all REMS participants must be trained and patients must be properly counseled

DISPENSING AND COUNSELING

PATIENT MEDICATION PROFILES

A pharmacy must keep medication profiles on all patients who have prescriptions filled at the pharmacy <u>except</u> when the pharmacist feels that the patient <u>will not come back to the pharmacy</u>. For example, a patient from another state or foreign country could be visiting California and is unlikely to return. The following information must be kept on a patient profile:[113]

- The patient's full name and address, telephone number, date of birth (or age) and gender.
- For each prescription dispensed by the pharmacy:
  - The drug name, strength, dosage form, route of administration (if other than oral), quantity and directions
  - The prescriber's name, license number, and if needed, the DEA registration number or other unique identifier
  - The date each drug was dispensed or refilled
  - The prescription number for each prescription

---

110   http://www.thalomidrems.com/ (accessed 2020 Nov 13)
111   https://www.ipledgeprogram.com/ (accessed 2020 Nov 13)
112   http://www.qsymiarems.com/ (accessed 2020 Nov 13)
113   CCR 1707.1

- Any of the following: allergies, idiosyncrasies, current medications and relevant prior medications, OTC medications, devices, social history or medical conditions, if provided.

- Any other information which the pharmacist, in his or her professional judgment, feels is appropriate to include.

The profile must be kept for at least <u>one year</u> from the date when the last prescription was filled.

DRUG UTILIZATION REVIEW

There are three types of drug utilization reviews (DURs):

- <u>Prospective DUR</u>: evaluation of a patient's medication profile <u>prior</u> to dispensing. This is performed by the <u>dispensing</u> pharmacist each time a prescription is filled.[114] The clerk at the window asks the patient if they have any new medications or allergies; if so, these will be added to the profile, and the pharmacist will review the current use to determine that the drug is safe to dispense. The purpose is to optimize the patient's therapy by looking for:

  - Therapeutic duplication

  - Incorrect dose

  - Incorrect treatment duration

  - Contraindications

  - Interactions between drugs, disease states or allergies

  - Abuse or diversion

- <u>Retrospective DUR</u>: review of drug therapy <u>after</u> the drug is <u>dispensed</u>. These are often conducted for many patients at once, and are performed by the state (according to the Omnibus Budget Reconciliation Act), a medical institution (e.g., hospital) or an insurance company.

- <u>Concurrent DUR</u>: on-going <u>monitoring during</u> the course of <u>treatment</u>. Regulations require hospital pharmacists to obtain a medication profile for each high-risk patient (as determined by the hospital). Technicians or interns can obtain the profile if they have received adequate training.[115]

PATIENT COUNSELING

Pharmacists must provide counseling (oral consultation) in any of the following situations:[116]

- The prescription drug has not been previously dispensed to the patient.

- The refill is being dispensed in a different dosage form, strength or with a new written prescription.

- If the patient requests counseling.

- When the pharmacist feels counseling is necessary.

---

114   CCR 1707.3
115   SB 1254
116   CCR 1707.2

The patient counseling must include at least the following items:[117]

- <u>Directions for use and storage</u>
- The <u>importance of compliance with directions</u>
- <u>Precautions and relevant warnings</u>, including common or severe side effects and interactions that can be encountered

When the pharmacist feels it is necessary, the patient counseling can also include:[118]

- The name and a description of the drug
- The route of administration
- The dose and/or the dosage form
- The duration of therapy
- Any special directions for use and storage
- Instructions on how to prepare the drug for administration
- Techniques for self-monitoring
- Refill information
- Additional adverse drug reactions or interactions
- What to do if a dose is missed

Only the <u>pharmacist</u> or <u>intern pharmacist</u> can make the <u>offer to counsel</u>. Although the offer to counsel must be made, the patient or patient's caregiver can refuse counseling. The pharmacist must provide patient counseling in an area suitable for <u>confidential patient consultation</u> to protect the patient's health information.

If the prescription is <u>mailed</u> or delivered, there must be a <u>written notice</u> that a pharmacist is available for patient consultation, the telephone number the patient can call and the hours of availability.[119] A pharmacist must be <u>available</u> for consultation for at least <u>six days of the week</u> and for at least <u>40 hours per week</u>.

Pharmacies often interact with patients with a limited grasp of the English language, and all patients need to know how to use their medications safely. In California, pharmacies are required to provide <u>interpretive services</u> in the patient's language during all hours that the pharmacy is open, either in person by the pharmacy staff who can communicate in the patient's language, or by the use of a third-party interpretive service available by telephone that is at or close to the pharmacy counter.[120] Communication concerns are discussed in the RxPrep NAPLEX Course Book chapter Answering Case-Based Exam Questions.

Pharmacists are not required by state law to counsel inpatients; however, a registered nurse, pharmacist or prescriber must provide discharge counseling.[121]

---

117   CCR 1707.2(c)
118   CCR 1707.2(d)
119   CCR 1707.2(b)(2)
120   CCR 1707.5(d)
121   B&PC 4074(e)

Ask Your Pharmacist!

California law requires a pharmacist to speak with you every time you get a **new** prescription.

You have the right to ask the pharmacist for:

Before taking your medicine, be sure you know:

1 The name of the medicine and what it does.

2 How and when to take it, for how long, and what to do if you miss a dose.

3 Possible side effects and what you should do if they occur.

4 Whether the new medicine will work safely with other medicines or supplements.

5 What foods, drinks, or activities should be avoided while taking the medicine.

Easy-to-read type
You have the right to ask for and receive from any pharmacy prescription drug labels in 12-point font.

Interpreter services
Interpreter services are available to you upon request at no cost.

Drug pricing
You may ask this pharmacy for information on drug pricing and use of generic drugs.

Ask the pharmacist if you have any questions.

This pharmacy must provide any medicine or device legally prescribed for you, unless:

• It is not covered by your insurance;

• You are unable to pay the cost of a copayment;

• The pharmacist determines doing so would be against the law or potentially harmful to health.

If a medicine or device is not immediately available, the pharmacy will work with you to help you get your medicine or device in a timely manner.

BE AWARE AND TAKE CARE:
Talk to your pharmacist!
CALIFORNIA STATE BOARD OF PHARMACY

1625 N. Market Blvd., Suite N-219 • Sacramento, CA 95834
(916) 574-7900 • www.pharmacy.ca.gov

Source: California Board of Pharmacy

NOTICE TO CONSUMERS

The purpose of the <u>Notice to Consumers</u> is to make sure consumers understand that they <u>have certain rights</u>, which includes the requirement to <u>receive counseling from a pharmacist</u> with each new prescription, the type of information that should be provided, and the patient's <u>right to ask questions</u> about their medications. The notice advises the patient that <u>easy-to-read type</u>, <u>interpreter services</u> and <u>drug prices</u> are available on request. The full-size poster of the Notice to Consumers (see previous page) must be posted in <u>public view</u> where it can be read by the consumer. The posters can be ordered on the board's website. Smaller versions can be printed out on legal size paper. The poster can be provided in languages that apply to the pharmacy's customer population. Alternatively, written receipts containing the required information can be provided to patients. This is an acceptable option for settings in which the patient does not physically see the pharmacist, such as mail-order or closed-door pharmacies. A pharmacy can also opt to display a PowerPoint presentation of the notice on a video screen.

HEALTH INSURANCE PORTABILITY AND ACCOUNTABILITY ACT

The <u>Health Insurance Portability and Accountability Act (HIPAA)</u> of 1996 created national standards to protect the <u>privacy</u> of a patient's health information (PHI). Healthcare facilities, insurance companies and pharmacies must ensure that <u>patient information is secure</u> and not available to viewers who do not require access, regardless of whether the information is in <u>electronic, verbal</u> or <u>written form</u>.

HIPAA outlines how <u>protected health information</u> (PHI) can be <u>shared by covered entities</u> and provides the patient the right to access their own information. Covered entities include:

- Healthcare professionals (e.g., <u>pharmacists</u>, doctors, dentists)
- Facilities where health care is provided (e.g., <u>pharmacies</u>, nursing homes, clinics)
- Health insurance companies

Healthcare professionals must have <u>documented HIPAA training</u> to learn how to protect patient PHI. <u>Violation</u> of HIPAA, either inadvertently or deliberately, can result in <u>fines and imprisonment</u>. An individual at each facility must be designated to enforce the privacy policy.

PROTECTED HEALTH INFORMATION (PHI)

PHI includes any individually identifiable health information that relates to:

- The patient's past, current or future physical or mental health (i.e., the medical record)
- The healthcare provided to the patient (e.g., laboratory tests, surgery, medications)
- The past, present or future payment for providing healthcare to the patient (e.g., hospital bills)
- When associated with health information:*
  - ❏ Name, address, birthdate, social security number

*If the identifying information is not related to health information, then it is not considered PHI. For example, names, residential addresses or phone numbers listed in a public directory such as a phone book are not PHI because there is no health data associated with it.

It is <u>permissible to share</u> PHI with:

- The <u>patient</u>

- Other <u>healthcare providers caring for</u> the patient

- Entities requiring the information for <u>payment or operational purposes</u> (e.g., care coordination, quality improvement)

- A limited data set can be provided for research, public health or institutional operations

- <u>Law enforcement</u>

  - Pursuant to a court order, warrant, subpoena or administrative request

  - To identify or locate a suspect, fugitive or missing person

  - In response to an information request about a victim (or suspected victim) of a crime

  - In response to criminal activity or a death related to criminal activity

- The <u>DEA, FDA</u>, medical board inspectors and pharmacy board <u>inspectors</u> (for a <u>public health purpose</u> or drug abuse concern)

- Organizations related to donation and transplantation of organs and tissues

If a release of PHI is not for the purposes listed above, the healthcare provider must receive the patient's <u>written authorization</u>. The authorization must be in <u>plain language</u> and include with <u>whom</u> the information will be shared, the <u>purpose</u>, the right to remove authorization, the <u>expiration date</u> and the <u>patient's signature</u>. If the patient is requesting the release, a written authorization is not necessary according to HIPAA, but some facilities will require it.

There must be <u>policies, procedures or protocols</u> in place for <u>disclosures</u> (routine, recurring or requests) to ensure that only the "<u>minimum necessary</u>" information required for the job or request is shared or used. This is designed to encourage the evaluation of who should be accessing PHI. For example, pharmacy support staff should only have access to the information required to complete their job tasks. Pharmacists can leave <u>voicemails</u> with the <u>minimum necessary information</u> on patients' home machines (e.g., "your medication is ready for pickup"). Prescriptions can be picked up by <u>family or friends</u> unless the pharmacist has reason to believe that this would be against the wishes of the patient.

<u>Incidental disclosures</u> are <u>unavoidable and acceptable</u> under HIPAA. Actions should be taken to minimize disclosure by speaking in a lower volume or speaking in a more private setting whenever possible. Examples of incidental disclosures include when someone overhears:

- <u>Oral coordination</u> of patient care at a nursing station

- A healthcare provider discussing a patient's condition over the phone with another provider, the patient or their family member

- A discussion between providers while on <u>rounds</u>

- A pharmacist discussing a prescription in person or over the phone with a patient or provider

To minimize disclosures, healthcare providers must be mindful of the following:

- Avoid discussing patient care in common areas (e.g., in elevators, cafeteria)
- Avoid posting any information about patients on social media (e.g., summaries of a case, pictures)
- Shred all documents before disposal; redaction (i.e., editing to censor/obscure content) is not an appropriate method of PHI destruction
- Cover patient identifiers on prescription bottles and bags before and during dispensing
- Close electronic medical records on computer screens when not in use and log out of the system
- Only access patient charts that are required for patient care

THE NOTICE OF PRIVACY PRACTICES

HIPAA requires a site-specific notice on the policies in place to protect PHI and with whom the information can be shared. This should be in simple language, and state the patient's rights to their own information and be specific that any release beyond what is stated in the policy will require the patient's approval. It should list the contact for the Department of Health & Human Services if the patient wishes to file a complaint, along with the contact for a person within the pharmacy if the patient wishes to discuss privacy concerns.

The HIPAA privacy notice should be placed in a prominent location within the pharmacy and on its website. It must be given to the patient on the first day that service is provided and at any other time it is requested. The pharmacy must make a good faith effort to obtain the patient's written acknowledgment of receiving the notice. The pharmacy must promptly revise and distribute its notice whenever there are changes to any of its privacy practices. A pharmacy can still provide services if the patient refuses to sign. The written acknowledgment must be separate from other signatures; one signature cannot be used to acknowledge receipt of the HIPAA privacy notice and to acknowledge another item, such as refusing the right to counsel. The signed HIPAA privacy disclosure forms must be kept for six years, and the patient has a right to request all of their privacy disclosures for the past six years.

The patient has the right to obtain a copy of their records. In California, patients must be able to inspect their medical records within five business days of making a written request, and receive copies within 15 business days. The maximum charge for copies is $0.25 cents/page, or $0.50 cents/page if the copies are being made from microfilm, plus the addition of reasonable clerical costs incurred in making the records available.[122] The patient can request a copy in the format of their choice (such as a printed copy or an electronic version sent via email).

---

122 H&SC 123110

DRUG SUBSTITUTION AND SELECTION

GENERIC SUBSTITUTION

A pharmacist can substitute generic, therapeutically-equivalent drugs for a branded drug using the FDA's _Approved Drug Products with Therapeutic Equivalence Evaluations_ (referred to as the _Orange Book)_ unless the prescriber or patient has requested otherwise. The drug must have the same active ingredients with the same strength, quantity and dosage form and the same generic drug name as determined by the United States Adopted Names (USAN), and accepted by the FDA.

The purpose of generic substitution is to provide the patient with a lower-cost drug while still providing the same therapeutic benefit. When a substitution is made, the cost savings from the switch must be communicated to the patient. If the generic equivalent is dispensed, the label must contain the generic name, the statement "generic for _____" where the brand name is inserted, and the manufacturer name (e.g., atorvastatin, generic for _Lipitor_, MFR: _Mylan Pharmaceuticals)._ If the brand is dispensed, only the brand name is required on the label.

The _Orange Book_ is available in print, online at the FDA website[123] or as a mobile application (_Orange Book Express)._

USING THE ORANGE BOOK

The Orange Book uses a two-letter code system. The first letter indicates if the drug is therapeutically equivalent to the reference listed drug (RLD) and the second letter provides additional information about the FDA's evaluation (e.g., route of administration or formulation).

If the first letter is A, then the drug is therapeutically equivalent to the RLD.

- AB-rated drugs had _in vivo_ (in the body) and/or _in vitro_ (outside the body, such as a test tube) studies completed that demonstrate bioequivalence.

  ❑ Most states permit brand drugs to be interchanged with AB-generics as a cost-savings measure.

- AA, AN (solutions or powder for aerosolization), AO (injectable oil solution), AP (injectable aqueous and non-aqueous solution) and AT-rated (topical) drugs are therapeutically equivalent to the RLD by meeting _in vitro_ bioequivalence, and they have no known _in vivo_ bioequivalence issues.

Three-character code

In some instances, a number is added to the end of the two letters to make a three-character code (e.g., AB1, AB2, AB3). Three-character codes are assigned when there is more than one RLD of the same strength under the same heading.

- For example, with levothyroxine, a generic dosage that has a three-character code can be used to substitute for three different branded drugs or RLDs with the same dose. In the image below, AB1 levothyroxine is therapeutically equivalent to other levothyroxine products that are rated AB1.

N021402	AB1,AB2	No	LEVOTHYROXINE SODIUM	TABLET; ORAL	0.025MG **See current Annual Edition, 1.8 Description of Special Situations, Levothyroxine Sodium	SYNTHROID	ABBVIE INC
N021402	AB1,AB2	Yes	LEVOTHYROXINE SODIUM	TABLET; ORAL	0.3MG **See current Annual Edition, 1.8 Description of Special Situations, Levothyroxine Sodium	SYNTHROID	ABBVIE INC
N021210	AB1,AB2,AB3	No	LEVOTHYROXINE SODIUM	TABLET; ORAL	0.025MG **See current Annual Edition, 1.8 Description of Special Situations, Levothyroxine Sodium	UNITHROID	JEROME STEVENS PHARMACEUTICALS INC
N021210	AB1,AB2,AB3	No	LEVOTHYROXINE SODIUM	TABLET; ORAL	0.05MG **See current Annual Edition, 1.8 Description of Special Situations, Levothyroxine Sodium	UNITHROID	JEROME STEVENS PHARMACEUTICALS INC

Orange book listing for some of the levothyroxine oral tablets.

A <u>substitution cannot be made</u> if the prescriber has taken any of the following actions:[124]

- Indicates, either orally, in handwriting or electronically "Do not substitute."
- Checks off a box pre-printed with the text "Do not substitute."
- Initials a box pre-printed with the text "Do not substitute."

SUBSTITUTING DRUG FORMULATIONS

A pharmacist can select a <u>different formulation</u> with the <u>same active ingredients</u> of <u>equivalent strength and duration of therapy</u> as the prescribed drug when the change will <u>improve patient compliance</u>. For example, if a pharmacist receives a prescription for ½ of the single strength sulfamethoxazole/trimethoprim tablets for a child, the pharmacist may suggest a 5 mL dose of the pediatric suspension to the child's parents. If the prescriber has indicated that no drug substitution is allowed, the formulation should not be changed.[125]

Formulations That Cannot be Switched

<u>Substitution is not permitted between long-acting and short-acting forms</u> of a medication with the same chemical ingredients. For example, the long-acting form of clonidine that is indicated for ADHD *(Kapvay)* cannot be interchanged with immediate-release clonidine.

Substitution is also <u>not permitted</u> between <u>combination drug products</u> and <u>multiple single agents</u>.[126] For example, a prescription for isosorbide dinitrate/hydralazine *(BiDil)* cannot be dispensed as the two individual drugs.

SUBSTITUTING BIOLOGICS

A <u>biosimilar</u> is considered "<u>highly similar</u>" to an <u>FDA-approved biologic</u> (known as a "<u>reference product</u>") and has no clinically meaningful difference. <u>Biosimilars are not considered therapeutically equivalent</u> to the reference product, so a pharmacist <u>cannot automatically substitute</u> these products for one another. Common biologics with approved biosimilars include filgrastim *(Neupogen)* with the biosimilar filgrastim-sndz *(Zarxio)*, and infliximab *(Remicade)* with the biosimilar infliximab-dyyb *(Inflectra)*.

Alternatively, interchangeable biosimilar products would be considered therapeutically equivalent to the reference product and could, by law, be substituted without contacting the prescriber. Many states, including California, have laws permitting the substitution of an FDA-approved interchangeable biosimilar for a reference product; however, there are currently no FDA-approved interchangeable biosimilar products.

When approved by the FDA, pharmacists will be able to dispense an interchangeable biosimilar product in place of the prescribed reference product, unless the prescriber indicates otherwise. The dispensed biosimilar product cannot cost more than the prescribed biologic product and the substitution must be communicated to the patient. The *Lists of Licensed Biological Products with Reference Product Exclusivity and Biosimilarity or Interchangeability Evaluations* (commonly referred to as *The Purple Book)* lists the reference products, biosimilar products and interchangeable products.

124   B&PC 4073(b)
125   B&PC 4052.5(a-b)
126   B&PC 4052.5 (f)

DRUG FORMULARIES

A formulary is a preferred drug list that a hospital or other institution, healthcare plan or PBM has chosen for their patients or members. The formulary should include the safest and most effective drugs according to current clinical guidelines/practices while considering cost. When similar drugs exist in a class, a competitive bidding process is used. For example, if a Pharmacy & Therapeutics (P&T) Committee wishes to select a prostaglandin analog for glaucoma, and five equally safe and effective drugs are on the market, the committee is likely to choose the least expensive option. Drugs may be removed from the formulary if there is a safety concern (e.g., sound-alike or look-alike, abuse potential) or if a less expensive drug is available.

The P&T Committee is responsible for all aspects of drug use in a healthcare system, which could be a small hospital or large pharmacy benefit manager (PBM). P&T members include physicians, pharmacists, nurses, administrators, quality improvement managers and the medication safety officer. The primary responsibilities of the P&T Committee are to create and update the formulary, conduct medication (or drug) use evaluations (MUE/DUE), monitor and report adverse drug events, conduct medication error safety initiatives (which will involve the medication safety officer) and develop clinical care plans and protocols.

Healthcare plans have formularies to outline which drugs will be covered in the outpatient or retail setting. These formularies have different tiers, which correlate with different copays. The typical outpatient formulary has three to five tiers; the lower the tier, the lower the copay. A copay is an out-of-pocket expense that the patient must pay in order to receive services such as doctor visits and prescription drugs. Specialty drugs, including biologics, will be placed on a high tier (such as tier 4 or 5), and the insurance plan may require prior authorization to use insurance coverage.

An example of formulary drug tiers for outpatient prescription medications:

TIER	TIER NAME	COST TO PATIENT (COPAY)
1	Generic drugs	$5 per prescription
2	Preferred brand drugs	$15 per prescription
3	Non-preferred brand drugs	$25 per prescription
4	Specialty drugs	10% copay, up to $250 maximum per prescription

THERAPEUTIC INTERCHANGE PROTOCOL

In healthcare facilities and some ambulatory care settings, therapeutic interchange protocols developed by the P&T Committee are used by pharmacists to dispense medications that are different, but therapeutically similar to the medication prescribed. The substituted drug is usually in the same pharmacological/therapeutic class. Therapeutic interchange protocols are a cost-effective strategy, so a more expensive drug can be interchanged with a less costly drug that provides a similar therapeutic benefit. Therapeutic interchange has become much more common in recent years because of the availability of multiple drugs in the same therapeutic class.

The pharmacist who substitutes one drug for another does <u>not</u> need to <u>discuss the change</u> with a <u>physician</u> as long as the substitution is established in the institution's therapeutic interchange <u>protocol</u>. Drug classes commonly included in therapeutic interchange protocols are <u>proton pump inhibitors, statins</u>, antacids, H2-blockers, hypnotics, ACE inhibitors, angiotensin receptor blockers, potassium supplements, antibiotics, insulins, topical steroids, laxatives and stool softeners.

Examples of therapeutic interchange include:

- Rosuvastatin *(Crestor)* is ordered and is not on the formulary: the pharmacist will select the therapeutically equivalent dose of a formulary drug (e.g., atorvastatin, simvastatin).
- Dexlansoprazole *(Dexilant)* is ordered and is not on the formulary, but pantoprazole is: the pharmacist will interchange *Dexilant* to a therapeutically equivalent dose of pantoprazole.

DISPENSING UNDER SPECIAL CIRCUMSTANCES

REFUSAL TO DISPENSE BASED ON RELIGIOUS, MORAL OR ETHICAL BELIEFS

In California, a pharmacist can refuse to dispense certain medications if <u>he or she has previously notified his or her employer, in writing</u> of their moral or conscientious objection. A written protocol must be established to ensure that the patient has <u>timely access</u> to the prescribed drug or device despite a pharmacist's refusal to dispense the prescription or order. This can mean having another staff pharmacist dispensing the drug or referring the patient to a nearby pharmacy.[127]

INTERNET PHARMACIES

There are two types of internet pharmacies: legitimate mail order pharmacies and rogue internet pharmacies. <u>Legitimate</u> mail order <u>pharmacies</u> dispense medications pursuant to a prescription from a <u>prescriber</u> who has <u>performed</u> a <u>good faith medical exam</u>. Internet prescriptions should only be dispensed to patients if the prescriber has performed an examination. Rogue online pharmacies sell drugs for non-medical purposes (e.g., recreational use) and do not require legitimate prescriptions.[128] These illegally operating pharmacies have contributed to the increase in controlled substance abuse and drug overdoses. In 2008, the Ryan Haight Online Pharmacy Consumer Protection Act was signed into law to <u>prevent illegal sales of controlled substances via the internet</u>. In order to legally dispense controlled substances through an online pharmacy, the pharmacy must register with the DEA and report their dispensing activity to the DEA.

TELEPHARMACY AT REMOTE SITES

Remote dispensing sites (i.e., telepharmacies) are permitted to operate in underserved locations that do not have an outpatient pharmacy within 10 miles.[129] A remote (<u>telepharmacy</u>) site is <u>managed by a supervising pharmacy</u> that is licensed and owns the remote pharmacy. The remote site is not licensed and is considered to be a satellite location of the licensed, supervising pharmacy. The pharmacist supervises all activities in the remote pharmacy (e.g., DUR, filling and counseling) with technology, such as audio-visual equipment.

127   *B&PC 733(b)(3)*
128   *B&PC 4067(a)*
129   *AB 401*

Requirements for a telepharmacy site:

- The supervising pharmacy and the remote site must be within 150 miles of each other.
- The pharmacist is not located at the remote site; <u>technicians</u> carry out the work, but can <u>only perform non-discretionary tasks</u>.
  - Technicians <u>cannot accept new prescriptions, compound medications</u> (which requires direct supervision), <u>or perform other discretionary tasks</u>.
  - A <u>single pharmacist</u> (off-site) can <u>supervise two technicians</u> who are working at the remote site.
  - A responsible <u>technician will have a key</u> to the remote site.
- <u>Counseling</u> for each prescription is <u>required</u> and must be done remotely by a pharmacist.
- Drugs are stored at the remote site, including controlled substances, and the PIC at the supervising site retains responsibility for controlled substances at the remote site.
  - <u>Controlled substances</u> must be <u>stored separately</u>.
  - All <u>management of controlled substances</u>, such as pulling them from the separate area, filling and dispensing, must be <u>captured on video</u>. The video recordings must be kept for at least <u>120 days</u>.
- The pharmacist must inventory the controlled substances when they are present at the remote site. At this time, the pharmacist should <u>countersign</u> for controlled substance deliveries.
- A <u>pharmacist</u> from the supervising pharmacy must <u>travel to the remote pharmacy</u> and conduct an inspection of the facility at least <u>once monthly</u>.

Pharmacy technicians must meet extra requirements in order to practice at a remote dispensing site. In addition to being licensed and certified, a technician must have one of the following:

- Associate's degree in pharmacy technology
- Bachelor's degree in any subject
- Certificate of completion from a board-approved course

An individual must also have completed at least 2,000 hours of experience as a pharmacy technician within the two years prior to beginning work at a remote site.

DISPENSING EPINEPHRINE AUTO-INJECTORS

A pharmacist can dispense <u>epinephrine auto-injectors</u> (e.g., *EpiPen*) to a <u>pre-hospital emergency medical care person</u> (e.g., paramedic), <u>lay rescuer</u> or <u>authorized entity</u> (e.g., ambulance company) for <u>first aid</u> purposes.[130, 131] The responder must obtain current certification that demonstrates they are trained and qualified to administer the auto-injector.

A physician must provide a <u>written order</u> specifying the quantity of epinephrine auto-injectors to be dispensed. A pharmacy can also provide auto-injectors for a <u>school district</u> or charter <u>school</u>, based on a physician/surgeon <u>written order</u>.[132]

---

130   B&PC 4119.3
131   B&PC 4119.4
132   B&PC 4119.2

Each epinephrine auto-injector should be dispensed with the manufacturer's product information sheet, and labeled with the following:

- The name of the person to whom the prescription was issued
- The designation "Section 1797.197a responder" and "First Aid Purposes Only"
- The dosage, use and expiration date

An individual that administers epinephrine in good faith to help someone experiencing anaphylaxis is given immunity from prosecution and no civil damages can be awarded.

DISPENSING BLOOD CLOTTING PRODUCTS FOR HOME USE

Hemophilia and Von Willebrand disease are hereditary bleeding disorders. Until the 1970s, people with severe hemophilia suffered from uncontrollable internal bleeding, orthopedic deformities and a shortened lifespan. More recently, the production of highly purified blood clotting factors has provided people with bleeding disorders the opportunity to lead normal lives. The preferred method of treatment of hemophilia today is intravenous injection, or infusion, of prescription blood clotting products at a federally designated regional hemophilia treatment center. Pharmacies and other entities specializing in the delivery of blood clotting products and related equipment, supplies and services for home use form a growing enterprise in California. Timely access to federally designated regional hemophilia centers and appropriate products/ services in the home reduces mortality and bleeding-related hospitalizations.

Each provider of blood clotting products for home use must:[133]

- Maintain 24-hour on-call service available every day of the year, screen telephone calls for emergencies and acknowledge all telephone calls within one hour.
- Have the ability to obtain all FDA-approved blood clotting products in multiple assay ranges (low, medium and high, as applicable) and vial sizes.
- Supply all necessary ancillary infusion equipment and supplies with each prescription, as needed.
- Ship the prescribed blood clotting products and ancillary infusion equipment and supplies to the patient within two business days.

DISPENSING DRUGS DURING A FEDERAL, STATE OR LOCAL EMERGENCY

Pharmacy law requirements can be waived during declared disasters and emergencies to ensure that patients receive medications. A pharmacist can dispense drugs (controlled and non-controlled) and devices in reasonable quantities without a prescription during a federal, state or local emergency.[134] A record containing the date, patient's name and address, and the drug or device name, strength and quantity dispensed must be maintained. The pharmacist must make a good faith effort to communicate this information to the patient's healthcare provider as soon as possible.

---

133   H&SC 125286.25
134   B&PC 4062

During a declared federal, state or local emergency, the board can allow the deployment of a mobile pharmacy in impacted areas in order to ensure the continuity of patient care, if all of the following conditions are met:

- The mobile pharmacy shares common ownership with at least one currently licensed pharmacy in good standing
- The mobile pharmacy retains records of dispensing
- A licensed pharmacist is on-site and managing the mobile pharmacy
- Reasonable security measures are taken to safeguard the drug supply maintained in the mobile pharmacy
- The mobile pharmacy is located within the declared emergency area or affected areas
- The mobile pharmacy ceases activity within 48 hours after the emergency is over

A recent example of this was in December 2017, when the president and the state governor declared a state of emergency due to the wildfires in southern California. Due to this emergency, the board allowed pharmacies in the affected areas to furnish residents with medically necessary drugs for themselves and their pets, without presentation of a prescription or drug container, even if prescriptions are not on file with the pharmacy.

If a pharmacy is damaged due to a natural disaster or declared emergency, it can relocate without being considered a transfer of ownership or location as long as the management and/or ownership have not changed.

DISPENSING AID-IN-DYING DRUGS

California's End of Life Option Act became effective in 2016. The end of life option can be referred to as death with dignity or physician-assisted suicide. The act permits mentally competent, terminally-ill adults to receive and voluntarily self-administer drugs to end their life in a peaceful, humane manner in a place and time of their choosing. Patients who wish to receive an aid-in-dying drug must be:

- ≥ 18 years of age
- A California resident
- Mentally competent (capable of making and communicating healthcare decisions for him/herself)
- Diagnosed with a terminal illness that will lead to death within six months (confirmed by two physicians)

The procedure to receive and use the medication is as follows:

1. The patient makes the first oral request to the physician. Patients who do not speak English can use a language interpreter. The physician must discuss the request for medication with the patient (and their interpreter, if applicable) alone to ensure that the request is voluntary.

2. After at least 15 days from the initial oral request, the patient makes a second oral request to the physician.

3. Anytime after the first oral request, a written request is given to the physician (the patient does not need to wait until after the second oral request to make the written request).

4. After the physician receives all three requests, the physician can furnish the drugs directly to the patient or send a prescription <u>directly</u> to a pharmacist. If the physician is sending a prescription to a pharmacy, the physician must contact the pharmacy first and inform the pharmacist of the prescription for aid-in-dying drugs. The physician must then personally <u>hand-deliver, mail or electronically send</u> the written prescription to the pharmacist. The patient is <u>never</u> in possession of the prescription.

5. The patient picks up the medication from the pharmacy or has it delivered.

6. The patient can change his/her mind about taking the medication at any time.

7. The patient must complete the final attestation form (to be given to the attending physician) within 48 hours before taking the medication.

The schedule II controlled substances <u>secobarbital</u> and <u>pentobarbital</u> are drugs that may be used for this purpose. The patient should be counseled on the importance of keeping the drug secure and out of the reach of children and pets. An anti-emetic should be taken an hour before the drug is taken. Secobarbital comes in capsules and pentobarbital comes in solution. If the contents of the capsules are opened, the drug can be mixed with juice to mask the bitter taste. A relative or caregiver must properly dispose of any unused drug by the patient. Unused drugs can be taken to a DEA-registered collection receptacle, a law-enforcement sponsored take-back event or by any other lawful means.

Death with dignity is a controversial issue as it goes against many healthcare providers' oath to do no harm. Pharmacists are not required to participate. A pharmacist can choose not to furnish the drugs due to conscientious, moral or ethical objection.[135]

AUTOMATED DRUG DELIVERY SYSTEMS

Automated drug delivery systems (ADDS) are cabinets that are used to store and dispense drugs to patients in skilled nursing and intermediate care facilities, hospital units and sometimes in other locations, such as medical clinics. An ADDS can also be referred to as an automated dispensing system (ADS) or an automated dispensing cabinet (ADC).

This section focuses on the use of the cabinets in skilled nursing or intermediate care facilities due to the lack of a pharmacy in most of these facilities, and the risk of diversion. If a patient is discharged, passes away or has a change of medication, unused drug can be diverted. If the ADDS is used to store and dispense <u>scheduled drugs</u>, a <u>DEA-registered</u> pharmacy must manage the cabinet. The California Board of Pharmacy requires that the system be under the control of a pharmacist and specifies how the cabinet should be stocked.

---

135   B&PC 733(b)(3)

For systems located in a skilled or intermediate care facility, the following is required:[136]

- The pharmacy and the nursing facility have policies and procedures to ensure that the drugs are being stored and dispensed properly.

- The pharmacist <u>reviews each medication order</u> and the patient's profile <u>before</u> the drug is removed from the ADDS. Use of an <u>override</u> to retrieve a medication before the pharmacist can review the order should be done in <u>emergency situations only</u>.

- When the cabinet is stocked directly in the facility, the stocking is done by a <u>pharmacist</u>.

- If the ADDS uses <u>removable</u> pockets, drawers or similar technology, the stocking is done outside the facility (i.e., at the pharmacy) and delivered back to the facility. With this type of stocking, the removable pockets or drawers must be transported between the pharmacy and the facility in a secure, <u>tamper-evident</u> container, and once the removable pockets or drawers are brought back to the pharmacy, they are restocked by a <u>pharmacist</u>, an <u>intern pharmacist</u> or a <u>technician</u> working under the supervision of a pharmacist.

The board is also concerned that drugs stored in an ADDS are properly labeled. The drugs must be labeled with at least the following information: drug name, strength and dosage form, manufacturer and manufacturer's lot number and expiration date.

Pharmacies that <u>remotely operate</u> an ADDS must <u>register the ADDS with the board</u> within 30 days of installing the device and annually as part of the license renewal. The pharmacy also has to inform the board in writing if the pharmacy discontinues operating the ADDS.[137] This includes pharmacies that remotely operate ADDS in long-term care facilities. Hospitals that operate an ADDS within their own facility do not need to register the ADDS separately with the board.[138]

REPACKAGING

REPACKAGING DRUGS IN ANTICIPATION OF RECEIVING PRESCRIPTIONS

Drugs can be pre-counted or poured (repackaged) from a bulk stock container into smaller quantities suitable for dispensing. This is often done for frequently used drugs so that the commonly dispensed drugs can be filled and dispensed quickly once the prescription is received. It may also be done for drugs that are not available at a reasonable cost in smaller quantities, or for drugs that are needed as unit-dose for a hospital or other type of institutional setting.

The repackaging should be done according to the Current Good Manufacturing Practices (CGMPs), and the drugs must be properly <u>labeled with at least the following information</u>: drug name, strength, dosage form, manufacturer's name and lot number, expiration date and quantity per repackaged unit. If the approved labeling contains instructions for handling or storage of the product, the repackaging will need to be done in accordance with those instructions. A log must be kept for drugs pre-packed for future dispensing.

---

136   H&SC 1261.6
137   B&PC 4105.5 (b)
138   B&PC 4105.5 (e)

CENTRALIZED HOSPITAL PACKAGING

The board has created a specialty license for a hospital pharmacy that performs centralized packaging for the pharmacy's hospital and <u>one or more general acute care hospitals</u> under <u>common ownership</u> and located <u>within a 75-mile radius</u> of each other. The centralized pharmacy can prepare and store a limited quantity of unit-dose drugs in advance of a patient-specific prescription in amounts necessary to ensure continuity of care.

Drugs packaged as single units or "unit-doses" help to reduce drug diversion, drug waste and medication errors. The unit-dose container is a non-reusable container designed to hold a quantity of drug intended for direct, oral administration as a single dose. Unit-dose packaging can be performed by the drug company or prepared from bulk containers in the pharmacy.

<u>Barcoding</u> is essential for medication safety since it helps to verify that the right drug is given to the right patient. The nurse administering the drug scans the barcode on the unit-dose medication and then scans the barcode on the patient's wristband to verify that it is the right drug, dose and route for the correct patient. Any unit-dose medication produced by a centralized hospital packaging pharmacy must be barcoded to be <u>machine readable</u> at the <u>inpatient's bedside</u> using barcode medication administration software. The software must read the barcode and compare the information retrieved to the electronic medical record of the inpatient.[139]

Unit-Dose Containers

The label for each unit-dose medication produced by a centralized hospital packaging pharmacy must contain all of the following:[140]

- Date that the medication was prepared
- Beyond-use date
- Name of the drug
- Quantity of each active ingredient
- Special storage or handling requirements
- Lot/control number assigned by the packaging pharmacy
  - A pharmacist must be able to retrieve the following information with the lot/control number: the components in each container and the expiration date and NDC of each drug component
- Name of the packaging pharmacy

Expiration Dates for Unit-Dose Containers

According to United States Pharmacopeia (USP) guidelines, the beyond-use date (BUD) for unit-dose containers is no later than either of the following:

- Six months from the date the drug is repackaged
- Expiration date on manufacturer's container

---

139   B&PC 4128.4
140   B&PC 4128.5

REPACKAGING PREVIOUSLY DISPENSED DRUGS INTO BLISTER PACKS

Drugs previously dispensed can be repackaged at the patient's request into a package that is more convenient for the patient.[141] This type of packaging is referred to as a "medication blister pack" or "bubble blister pack" or "medication pill card." This can be done when a patient has a complicated drug regimen and/or lives in a long-term care facility. Repackaging a patient's drugs into a bubble pack could increase compliance and reduce medication errors.

Any pharmacy providing repackaging services must have policies and procedures for the repackaging process, and must label the repackaged drugs with the following:

- All the information required for a prescription label.[142]

- The name and address of the pharmacy that initially dispensed the drugs to the patient, and the name and address of the pharmacy repackaging the drugs, if different.

COMPOUNDING

Pharmacies engaged in compounding must comply with the United States Pharmacopeia (USP) compounding standards, in addition to any regulations set by the California Board of Pharmacy. For more information regarding the USP standards, please see the Compounding chapters in the RxPrep NAPLEX Course Book.

SECTION 503A – TRADITIONAL COMPOUNDING

Compounding is the process of combining or altering ingredients to create a medication. A traditional compounded drug is prepared by a pharmacist for an individual patient based on a prescription. Compounded drugs meet unique needs and are not FDA-approved. The dose or formulation cannot be commercially available. Traditional compounding is used for this purpose and is defined under section 503A of the Drug Quality and Security Act (DQSA).

Traditional compounding includes any of the following:[143]

- Altering the dosage form or delivery system
- Altering the strength
- Combining components or active ingredients
- Preparing a drug product from chemicals or bulk drug substances

These activities are not defined as compounding:[144]

- Reconstituting a drug, according to the manufacturer's directions
- Splitting tablets
- Adding flavoring agents to an existing drug product in order to enhance palatability

---

141   B&PC 4052.7
142   B&PC 4076
143   CCR 1735(a)
144   CCR 1735(b)

Drugs made with traditional compounding methods have three <u>exemptions</u> from requirements that otherwise apply to prescription drugs:

- Complying with the FDA's Current Good Manufacturing Practices (CGMPs)

- Labeling with adequate directions for use

- The need to complete a New Drug Application (NDA) in order to have the end product FDA-approved

Section 503A permits pharmacists to prepare small batches of a compounded preparation in advance if the dispensing history of the pharmacy supports the need. If a pharmacist in a medical building prepares 3 – 4 prescriptions of the same strength of a progesterone cream each day, the pharmacy can prepare a few days' supply of the cream so it is ready when the prescriptions are received. These preparations will need to be labeled with the appropriate BUD.

Pharmacies can sell a reasonable quantity of compounded preparations to prescribers for <u>administration</u> or <u>application</u> to patients (human and animal) in the <u>prescriber's office</u>.[145] Prescribers <u>cannot</u> purchase compounded preparations from pharmacies to <u>furnish/dispense</u> to human patients. The prescriber's office will need to send a <u>purchase order</u> or other <u>documentation</u> to the pharmacy that <u>lists the patients</u> requiring the preparation. The <u>quantity</u> needed for each patient should be specified. The preparations are delivered to the prescriber's office and signed for by the prescriber or their agent.

Veterinarians can also purchase compounded preparations from a pharmacy for the purpose of <u>furnishing/dispensing</u> up to a <u>120-hour supply</u> of compounded preparations to their patients (i.e., <u>animals</u>).[146] This means a veterinarian can administer the compounded preparation to the animal in the office and/or provide a take-home supply. When veterinarians order compounded preparations from the pharmacy, the veterinarians must indicate how many veterinary patients they anticipate needing the compound for and must also indicate how much they anticipate using per veterinary patient (for office-use and for furnishing).

Pharmacies can also compound <u>patient-specific parenteral therapy</u> for other pharmacies. For example, one pharmacy receives the prescription/order and dispenses the preparation but contracts with another pharmacy to prepare the compound.[147] Compounding can only begin after receiving a patient-specific prescription/order. The <u>label</u> on the dispensed compound must include the <u>name of both</u> the <u>compounding</u> pharmacy and the <u>dispensing</u> pharmacy.

SECTION 503B – OUTSOURCING FACILITIES

In 2012, contaminated methylprednisolone injections prepared by the New England Compounding Center (NECC) caused a fungal meningitis outbreak. Over 700 fungal infections and 64 deaths occurred nationwide. The vials of compounded methylprednisolone were contaminated due to unsanitary conditions and poor aseptic technique. Adequate regulations and oversight of compounding pharmacies were not in place to proactively identify the problem.

145   CCR 1735.2(c)
146   CCR 1735.2(c)(3)
147   B&PC 4123

As a result, the FDA revised the Drug Quality and Security Act, dividing compounding pharmacies into two groups: <u>503A</u> and <u>503B</u> facilities.[148]

Section 503B permits specially licensed compounding facilities to operate as an outsourcing facility. These facilities can prepare <u>bulk medications without</u> patient-specific <u>prescriptions</u> as long as the facility meets certain requirements. This is especially important in the event of drug shortages. To register as an outsourcing facility under 503B, the facility needs to be compounding <u>sterile</u> drugs for <u>humans</u>.

Facilities can operate as an outsourcing facility if the following requirements are met:

- The drugs must be compounded in compliance with CGMPs.
- The facility is licensed as an outsourcing facility by the <u>FDA</u> and the <u>California Board of Pharmacy</u>.[149]
- It <u>cannot be licensed as a sterile compounding pharmacy</u> at the same time.
- It <u>cannot perform the functions of a pharmacy</u>, such as dispensing patient-specific prescriptions.[150]
- It is subject to <u>inspection</u> by the FDA and California Board of Pharmacy.[151]
- The preparations must be made by or under the supervision of a licensed <u>pharmacist</u>.
- The facility must meet certain labeling requirements, drug reporting requirements and adverse event reporting requirements.

MANUFACTURING VERSUS COMPOUNDING

	MANUFACTURING	TRADITIONAL (503A) COMPOUNDING	OUTSOURCING (503B) COMPOUNDING
Regulation	FDA	State board	FDA, state board
Standards	FDA drug approval USP CGMPs	503A USP	503B USP CGMPs
Individual Prescription Required	No	Yes	No
Interstate Distribution	Yes	Up to 5% of total sales (the "5% rule")	Yes

148 https://www.fda.gov/drugs/human-drug-compounding/compounding-laws-and-policies (accessed 2020 Nov 13)
149 B&PC 4129
150 B&PC 4129(e)
151 B&PC 4129.1(c), B&PC 4129.2(c)

HANDLING HAZARDOUS DRUGS

The National Institute for Occupational Safety and Health (NIOSH) issues a list of hazardous drugs (HDs) that require special precautions in order to prevent work-related injury and illness. HDs can cause harm to healthcare staff who handle them, including pharmacists, technicians, nurses and cleaning staff. Common HDs include antineoplastics (chemotherapy drugs), teratogenic drugs, hormones and transplant drugs. The standard for handling drugs on the NIOSH list are set by USP in Chapter 800. The California Board of Pharmacy has implemented regulations that closely mirror the USP 800 standards.[152] Minimally, a pharmacy or other setting handling HDs must have the following:

- Engineering controls, such as closed-system transfer devices and negative pressure ventilated cabinets (e.g.,hood or biological safety cabinets).
  - ❏ The hood externally vents the drug's toxic fumes, with a negative air pressure inside the hood (air moves away from the staff near the hood).
- Personal protective equipment (e.g., chemotherapy gown, respiratory protection, goggles, two pairs of shoe covers, chemotherapy gloves).
  - ❏ HDs will require either single or double gloves when handling. Sterile HD compounding requires double gloves. The outer pair must be sterile. Per USP 800, gloves for all HD compounding should be powder-free because the powder can contain HD residue.
- Safe work practices, spill kits and disposal requirements.

For more information, refer to the Compounding chapters in the RxPrep NAPLEX Course Book.

NUCLEAR PHARMACY

Nuclear pharmacists compound and dispense radioactive drugs for diagnostic purposes or treatment. Due to the inherent danger of radioactive exposure and the need to reduce exposure with known techniques, pharmacists handling radioactive drugs must be competent in the preparation, storage and dispensing of radioactive drugs.[153] A pharmacist qualified in radioactive drug management must be in the pharmacy whenever radioactive drugs are being provided to medical staff. All personnel involved in the furnishing of radioactive drugs must be under the immediate and direct supervision of a qualified nuclear pharmacist. Pharmacies that compound nuclear drugs must have a sterile compounding permit from the board.

152   CCR Articles 4.5, 7 and 7.5
153   CCR 1708.4

PHARMACY PRACTICE PART 2:
FURNISHING, ADMINISTERING AND CLINICAL SERVICES

CHAPTER CONTENTS

Test Ordering, Interpretation and Management **66**
Furnishing and Administering Drugs & Devices **67**
    Administering Injectable Drugs and Biologics 67
    Initiating and Administering Immunizations 68
    Furnishing Emergency Contraception 69
    Furnishing Naloxone 72
    Furnishing Prescription Nicotine Replacement Therapy 74
    Furnishing Self-Administered Hormonal Contraceptives 75
    Furnishing Travel Medications 77
    Furnishing Pre-Exposure Prophylaxis (PrEP) 78
    Furnishing Post-Exposure Prophylaxis (PEP) 79
Providing Clinical Services **79**
    CLIA-Waived Tests 79
    Physical Assessments 80
    Health Screenings 84
Quality Assurance Programs **86**
    National Patient Safety Goals 86
    Standard Order Sets 86
    Antimicrobial Stewardship Programs 87
    Medication Utilization Evaluations 87
    Peer Review and Self-Evaluation 88
    Medication Error Reporting 88
Promoting Public Health **89**
    Medicare Part D 89
    Covered California 90
    Patient Assistance Programs 90
    Tablet Splitting 91
    Other Drug Cost-Saving Strategies 91

PHARMACY PRACTICE PART 2:
FURNISHING, ADMINISTERING AND CLINICAL SERVICES

TEST ORDERING, INTERPRETATION AND MANAGEMENT

The California Pharmacists Association has developed guidelines for pharmacists ordering and managing tests to ensure safe and appropriate medication therapy.[154] The key principles are reviewed below:

- Testing should be for ensuring safe and effective medication therapy in coordination with the patient's PCP or with the diagnosing prescriber.

- Tests must only be ordered when necessary.

- Test results must be managed appropriately and promptly, and patients should receive feedback on their tests in a timely manner.

- Quality assurance should be integrated into the processes for test ordering, interpretation and management.

Pharmacists are individually responsible for personal competence in ordering tests and interpreting results. Variables that may impact test results must be considered when interpreting results, including timing of testing, medications, renal or hepatic function, fluid status and lab error. Examples of appropriate tests for a pharmacist to order include:

- Serum levels for narrow therapeutic index drugs (e.g., antiarrhythmics, antipsychotics, anticonvulsants)

- INR for patients taking warfarin

- Renal and hepatic function tests for patients taking medications requiring renal or hepatic dose adjustments

- Culture and sensitivity results for selection of appropriate antibiotic therapy

Pharmacists who order tests should be available, or have back-up available, to respond promptly to critical results. At a minimum, a pharmacist should relay the critical value to the provider with primary responsibility for that aspect of the patient's care. Critical values must be reported in the time frame indicated in the protocol for management of the condition, if present. If a test result

154   https://cpha.com/wp-content/uploads/2017/09/Guidelines-for-pharmacists-ordering-tests-in-California-5-0.pdf (accessed 2020 Nov 13)

does not appear reasonable, it should be repeated. Pharmacists should refer patients to other healthcare professionals as problems are identified that require additional care.

All actions related to test ordering, interpretation and management, including changes in drug treatment, must be <u>documented within 24 hours</u> in a system accessible to the healthcare team members. Preferably, the <u>Electronic Health Record (EHR)</u> should be available to the pharmacist. A large benefit with the use of EHRs is a reduction in unnecessary or duplicate testing.

Pharmacists should include each of the following items when they document changes in care:

- Interpretation of the result
- Rationale for the decision
- Information provided to the patient and the healthcare team members

A quality assurance (QA) assessment should be used to document the quality of the pharmacist's care.

FURNISHING AND ADMINISTERING DRUGS & DEVICES

ADMINISTERING INJECTABLE DRUGS AND BIOLOGICS

Prior to SB 493, pharmacists could administer only oral and topical drugs that had been ordered by a prescriber, and pharmacists who were trained in immunizations could administer vaccines. The passing of SB 493 allows pharmacists to administer drugs and biologics by other routes, including by injection. Pharmacists who wish to administer drugs or vaccines must receive <u>adequate training</u> in the possible routes of administration.

In adults, intramuscular <u>(IM) injections</u> are given in the <u>deltoid muscle</u> at the central and thickest portion above the level of the armpit and below the acromion. Emerging evidence suggests providers may be giving IM vaccines too high on the deltoid; make sure to give in the thickest, most central part of the deltoid. <u>Adults require a 1" needle</u> (or a 1½" needle for women greater than 200 pounds or men greater than 260 pounds). Use a $22 - 25$ gauge needle inserted at a 90 degree angle. The higher the gauge, the thinner the needle. <u>Subcutaneous (SC) injections</u> are given in the <u>fatty tissue over the triceps with a 5/8"</u>, $23 - 25$ gauge needle at a <u>45 degree angle</u>.

Multiple injections given in the same extremity should be separated by a minimum of 1 inch, if possible. For patients that require frequent injections, SC and IM injection sites are rotated to avoid irritation. In most cases, the concurrent use of injectable vasoconstrictors is not recommended due to the risk of abscess, except when localized drug administration is desired (e.g., epinephrine and lidocaine for anesthesia within a localized area).

Some injectable drugs can be absorbed faster with heat or massage. For example, the instructions for *EpiPen* administration include massaging the area for 10 seconds after injecting. With drugs that can cause easy bruising, such as anticoagulants, it is important not to massage the area.

With all injections, there must be an emergency protocol to treat severe reactions as described in the RxPrep NAPLEX Course Book Immunizations chapter. The pharmacy will need to have an additional protocol for needle-stick injuries. Safe syringe disposal must be practiced, which is discussed in the Medication Safety & Quality Improvement chapter of the RxPrep NAPLEX Course Book.[155]

INITIATING AND ADMINISTERING IMMUNIZATIONS

Pharmacists in California can independently administer <u>routine</u> immunizations to adults and children ages <u>three years</u> and older.[156] The routine immunizations are those recommended by the Advisory Committee on Immunization Practices (ACIP) and published by the Centers for Disease Control and Prevention (CDC). A physician-directed protocol may be used if administering non-routine immunizations. A pharmacist can also initiate and administer <u>epinephrine</u> or <u>diphenhydramine</u> by injection to treat a severe allergic reaction.

Pharmacists and interns who initiate and administer vaccines must:

- Complete a CDC or ACIP-approved <u>immunization training program</u>
- Maintain <u>basic life support certification</u>
- Complete <u>one hour</u> of continuing education on immunizations and vaccines every <u>two years</u>

In order for <u>intern pharmacists</u> to <u>administer</u> vaccines, <u>both</u> the <u>supervising pharmacist</u> and the <u>intern</u> must have <u>completed</u> an approved immunization <u>training</u> program. This is true for other activities that require special training or certification. If the pharmacist is not trained or certified in the activity, they will not be able to adequately supervise interns performing the activity.

The pharmacist must also comply with the following recordkeeping and reporting requirements:

- Pharmacists must notify each patient's <u>primary care provider</u> (PCP) and each pregnant patient's <u>prenatal care provider</u> (if applicable) within <u>14 days</u> of the administration of any vaccine. If the patient does not have a PCP, the pharmacist should advise the patient to consult with a healthcare provider of their choice.
- Pharmacists must report the administration of any vaccine to the <u>California Immunization Registry</u> (CAIR). Pharmacies (not pharmacists) must be enrolled in CAIR. It is optional for individual pharmacists to enroll in CAIR.
- A <u>patient vaccine administration record</u> must be kept and readily retrievable during the pharmacy's normal business hours. A pharmacist must provide each patient with a vaccine administration record.

Effective January 2016, all children (kindergarten to 12th grade) in public or private schools (i.e., not home-schooled) must be immunized prior to admittance. Medical exemptions may be permitted, but personal belief exemptions have been eliminated.[157] Schools should be able to review the student vaccination history on the immunization registry.

155   http://www.immunize.org/catg.d/p2020.pdf (accessed 2020 Nov 13)
156   B&PC 4052.8
157   SB 277

FURNISHING EMERGENCY CONTRACEPTION

The two types of medications approved for emergency contraception (EC) are <u>levonorgestrel</u> and <u>ulipristal</u>. Alternatively, a pharmacist can furnish <u>high-dose birth control pills</u> off-label to be used as EC.[158] *Plan B One-Step* and its generic equivalents are administered as a single dose of levonorgestrel 1.5 mg. Ulipristal *(Ella)* is a single dose, one-tablet EC product available only by <u>prescription</u>. Levonorgestrel and ulipristal have similar efficacy during the first <u>72 hours</u> (three days) after unprotected intercourse. Levonorgestrel and ulipristal can both be recommended for up to <u>120 hours</u> (five days), but ulipristal is more effective from 72 – 120 hours (3 – 5 days) after unprotected intercourse. EC has not been shown to harm a developing fetus and does not impair a woman's ability to conceive in the future. If a woman has taken EC and does not have a menstrual period within three weeks, she should take a pregnancy test.

EC can be obtained in one of three ways:

1. Over-the-counter (OTC)

2. Prescription

3. Furnished by a pharmacist in California under the board's EC protocol

OTC Option

Plan B One-Step and similar products can be purchased <u>OTC, without sex, age or identification requirements</u>. The FDA requests that OTC levonorgestrel products be placed in the aisle with other family planning items, such as condoms and spermicide. This placement allows customers to purchase EC even when a pharmacist is not on duty. EC can be purchased at any time the store is open, including times when the pharmacy department is closed.

Prescription Option

A prescriber can issue a prescription for EC to a patient. If a <u>prescription is received</u>, the pharmacist can process it through insurance and dispense it as they would other prescription drugs. The Affordable Care Act (ACA) requires coverage for "essential health services." This includes "women's preventive services" (e.g., contraception, EC) with no cost-sharing for the patient. Under the ACA, EC is covered only with a <u>prescription</u> written for a <u>female</u> patient.[159],[160] The only insurance plans under

© Minerva Studio/Shutterstock.com

the ACA (which can be found in the health insurance marketplace called *"Covered California"*) that may not cover EC are grandfathered health plans (which have been permitted to retain some of their original features for a set time period) or religiously-exempt employer health plans.

158   https://www.cdc.gov/reproductivehealth/contraception/mmwr/spr/emergency.html#type (accessed 2020 Nov 13)
159   https://www.gpo.gov/fdsys/pkg/FR-2013-07-02/pdf/2013-15866.pdf (accessed 2020 Nov 13)
160   http://www.hrsa.gov/womensguidelines/(accessed 2020 Nov 13)

Procotol Option

A pharmacist can <u>furnish</u> EC under the board's protocol.[161] A patient might choose this option if she does <u>not have a prescription</u> from a prescriber and <u>wishes to use insurance coverage</u>. In order to furnish EC under the protocol, the pharmacist must have completed <u>one hour</u> of CE on EC. The pharmacist must ask and communicate the following to the patient:

- Are you <u>allergic</u> to any medications?

- Timing is an essential element of the product's effectiveness. Emergency contraception should be taken as soon as possible after unprotected intercourse. Treatment can begin up to <u>five days (120 hours)</u> after unprotected intercourse.

- Emergency contraception use <u>will not interfere with an established or implanted pregnancy</u>.

- If more than 72 hours have elapsed since unprotected intercourse, the use of *Ella* may be preferred. For other emergency contraception options, consult with your healthcare provider.[162]

- Please follow up with your healthcare provider after the use of emergency contraception.

EC can be furnished for <u>future use</u>, meaning a patient can receive a supply to keep on hand in the event that unprotected intercourse occurs in the future. There are no product quantity limits.

A Fact Sheet (see image on the following page) must be provided to the patient when furnishing EC.[163] The board's website provides the Fact Sheet in 10 languages. The pharmacist should answer any questions the patient may have and record the necessary information in the patient's medication record as required for any prescription. If a pharmacist has a reasonable belief that the patient will not continue to obtain prescriptions from that pharmacy, such as an out-of-town patient who is visiting the area, a medication profile is not required.[164]

The pharmacy should maintain an inventory of EC medications and adjunctive OTC medications (e.g., meclizine, dimenhydrinate) indicated for nausea and vomiting (N/V). There is a higher incidence of N/V with estrogen-containing EC compared to levonorgestrel (progestin-only) formulations. Patients will need to be given information concerning dosing and potential adverse effects. Medication for N/V should be taken 30 – 60 minutes before the EC dose.

A pharmacist can provide up to 12 non-spermicidal condoms to each Medi-Cal and Family Planning, Access, Care and Treatment (PACT) beneficiary who obtains EC. Medi-Cal and Family PACT are programs for low-income residents of California. Family PACT focuses on family planning and provides contraception coverage.

If a pharmacist refuses to dispense EC, the pharmacy must have a protocol in place to ensure that the patient has timely access to the drug.[165] If EC is not immediately available at the pharmacy (e.g., if it is out of stock or if the only pharmacist on duty refuses to dispense it), the pharmacist will need to refer the patient to another EC provider.

161   CCR 1746
162   A copper intrauterine device (IUD) can be inserted within five days of unprotected intercourse, and will provide the benefit of ongoing contraception.
163   http://www.pharmacy.ca.gov/publications/emer_contraception.pdf (accessed 2020 Nov 13)
164   CCR 1707.1(a)
165   CCR 1746(b)(5), B&PC 733(b)(3)

Key Facts About Emergency Contraception

Emergency Contraception (EC) is a safe and effective way to prevent pregnancy after sex.

Consider using Emergency Contraception (EC) if:

- You had unprotected sex, or
- You think your contraceptive didn't work.

What are Emergency Contraceptive pills?

Emergency Contraceptive pills contain the same medication as regular birth control pills, and help to prevent pregnancy. There are three basic types of Emergency Contraceptive pills:

- Progestin-only pills (Plan B® One-Step, Next Choice®)
- Ulipristal acetate (ella®)
- High doses of regular oral contraceptive pills

Don't wait! Take EC as soon as possible.

- It is best to take EC as soon as possible; the sooner you take EC the more effective it is.
- It has been shown to be effective for up to 5 days.
- For more information talk to your pharmacist or doctor.

When taken as directed Emergency Contraception has been shown to be safe and effective.

- Emergency Contraception may reduce the risk of pregnancy by up to 89 percent.
- The effectiveness of EC varies based on the type used and when it is taken.
- EC is only recommended as a backup and should not be used as your primary method of birth control.
- Emergency Contraceptive pills do not protect against sexually transmitted infections, including HIV/AIDS.

What EC does:

- Emergency Contraceptive pills prevent pregnancy.
- Emergency Contraceptive pills are not effective after pregnancy has occurred and they will not harm the developing fetus.
- Emergency Contraceptive pills are NOT the same as RU-486 (the abortion pill).
- Using Emergency Contraceptive pills will not affect a woman's ability to become pregnant in the future.

Follow-up after taking Emergency Contraceptive pills:

- If you vomit after taking emergency contraception you may need to take another dose. Before you do, contact a pharmacist or healthcare provider immediately.
- If you do not get a normal period within three weeks, take a pregnancy test.
- It is important to visit your doctor or clinic for a regular birth control method and information about preventing sexually transmitted infections.
- Medical providers or your pharmacist can provide Emergency Contraception for future use if needed.

In California, women and men may receive free family planning services through Family PACT based on income.

If you don't have a doctor or clinic, call (800) 942-1054 to find a Family PACT provider near you.

Under the Affordable Care Act (ACA), Emergency Contraception may be covered with a prescription.

BE AWARE AND TAKE CARE: Talk to your pharmacist!
CALIFORNIA STATE BOARD OF PHARMACY

California State Board of Pharmacy
1625 North Market Blvd., Suite N-219
Sacramento, CA 95834

www.pharmacy.ca.gov
(916) 574-7900

Source: California Board of Pharmacy

FURNISHING NALOXONE

The rising death toll due to inappropriate/excessive opioid use has spurred a national movement to make naloxone more widely available to the public. Naloxone is an <u>opioid antagonist</u> that binds to and displaces the opioid from its receptor sites. Naloxone reverses the action of the opioid, including <u>overdose</u> symptoms and analgesia. In chronic users, the abrupt reversal with naloxone will cause <u>opioid withdrawal</u> symptoms, which can be severe.

The statewide protocol covers the use of <u>FDA-approved naloxone formulations</u>, including the injection and nasal spray *(Narcan)*. Naloxone can be given if opioid overdose is <u>suspected</u> due to respiratory symptoms and/or symptoms of CNS depression. Prescribers must now <u>offer naloxone</u>.

If naloxone is administered, 911 must be called since emergency care will be required. Symptoms of opioid overdose include:

- Extreme or unusual somnolence (cannot be awakened verbally or with a firm sternal rub)
- Respiratory difficulty, ranging from slow or shallow breathing to complete respiratory arrest
- Miosis (very small "pinpoint" pupils)
- Bradycardia

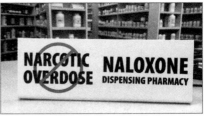

🖼 *PureRadiancePhoto/Shutterstock.com*

Pharmacists Furnishing Naloxone Pursuant to Board Protocol

California pharmacists can furnish naloxone without a prescription pursuant to the protocol and billed to Medi-Cal, Medicare Part B or private insurance. A pharmacist must complete <u>one hour</u> of CE on the use of naloxone or an equivalent curriculum-based training program from a board-recognized school of pharmacy. The board also provides a free webinar training program.

Naloxone should be offered to those who request it (e.g., those on opioids or their friends/family members) and opioid users at the highest risk for overdose. The <u>highest risk</u> criteria include:

- History of a <u>prior overdose</u>
- Use of ≥ 50 morphine milligram equivalents (MME) per day (convert the home opioid daily dose to morphine if using a different opioid)
- Concurrent <u>benzodiazepine</u> use
- A recent period of opioid abstinence
- Chronic illness that affects the lung, liver or kidney

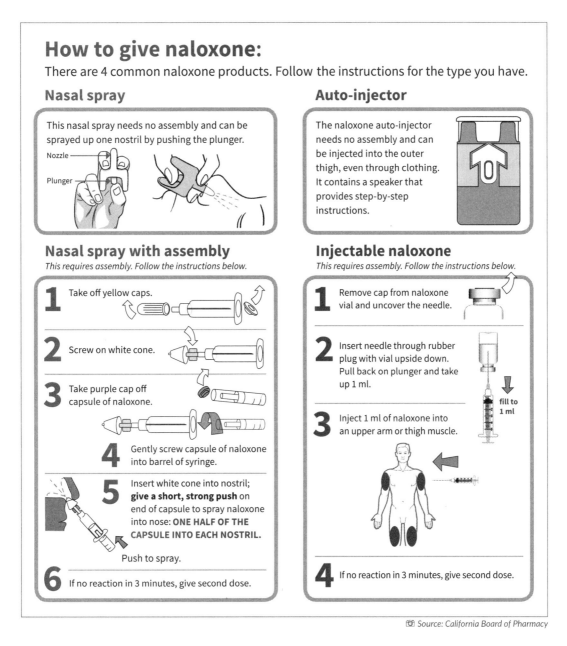

Source: California Board of Pharmacy

Pharmacists furnishing naloxone according to the protocol must follow these steps[166,167]:

- Ask if the recipient uses opioids or knows someone who does.

- Ask if the recipient has a known naloxone hypersensitivity.

- Provide the recipient with training in opioid overdose prevention, recognition, response and the administration of naloxone. When dispensing naloxone, <u>patient counseling cannot be waived</u>. It is best to avoid the word "overdose" when discussing naloxone with patients and family members. "Toxicity" and "antidote" are preferable.

- Provide the board-approved Fact Sheet.

- With the patient's permission, the pharmacist must notify the patient's PCP that naloxone was furnished.

- Keep records of furnishing the naloxone for <u>three years</u>.

166   http://www.pharmacy.ca.gov/publications/naloxone_protocol.pdf (accessed 2020 Nov 13)
167   http://www.pharmacy.ca.gov/publications/naloxone_fact_sheet.pdf (accessed 2020 Nov 13)

Pharmacies Furnishing Naloxone to Schools Pursuant to a Prescription

Pharmacies can furnish naloxone to a <u>school district, county office of education</u> or <u>charter school</u> pursuant to a prescriber's <u>prescription</u>.[168, 169] School nurses and trained volunteers can administer the naloxone to treat opioid overdose.

FURNISHING PRESCRIPTION NICOTINE REPLACEMENT THERAPY

<u>Tobacco dependence</u> is a chronic illness that typically requires repeated interventions and multiple attempts to quit. Effective treatments exist that can significantly increase rates of long-term abstinence.[170]

There are several OTC tobacco cessation products that pharmacists can recommend to patients without requiring a prescription (e.g., nicotine patch, gum and lozenges). The California Board of Pharmacy has a standing protocol that allows pharmacists to furnish <u>prescription nicotine replacement therapy (NRT)</u>, including the <u>inhaler</u> and <u>nasal spray</u>. A pharmacist can furnish these products once they complete a minimum of <u>two hours</u> of an approved CE program specific to smoking cessation therapy and NRT, or an equivalent curriculum-based training program within the last two years at an accredited California school of pharmacy. The pharmacist must complete ongoing CE focused on smoking cessation therapy every <u>two years</u>. Prior to selecting and furnishing NRT, the pharmacist must screen the patient using the following criteria and questions[171]:

- Review the patient's current tobacco use and past quit attempts.
- Ask the patient a series of screening questions:
  - Are you <u>pregnant</u> or planning to become pregnant? (If yes, do not furnish and refer to an appropriate healthcare provider.)
  - Have you had a <u>heart attack</u> within the last two weeks? (If yes, furnish with caution and refer to an appropriate healthcare provider.)
  - Do you have any history of <u>heart palpitations, irregular heartbeats</u>, or have you been diagnosed with a serious <u>arrhythmia</u>? (If yes, furnish with caution and refer to an appropriate healthcare provider.)
  - Do you currently experience frequent <u>chest pain</u> or have you been diagnosed with <u>unstable angina</u>? (If yes, furnish with caution and refer to an appropriate healthcare provider.)
  - Do you have any history of allergic rhinitis (e.g., <u>nasal allergies</u>)? (If yes, <u>avoid nasal spray</u>.)
  - Have you been diagnosed with temporal mandibular joint (<u>TMJ) dysfunction</u>? (If yes, <u>avoid nicotine gum</u>.)
- Counsel patients on therapy and refer patients for further smoking cessation support.

---

168   B&PC 4119.8
169   Education Code 49414.3
170   Review the RxPrep NAPLEX Course Book Tobacco Cessation chapter
171   CCR 1746.2

- Notify the patient's PCP of the drugs or devices provided or enter the information in a shared patient record system. If the patient does not have a PCP, the pharmacist should provide the patient with a written record of what they received, and advise the patient to consult a PCP of their choice.

- The records of furnishing the NRT are kept for <u>three years</u>.

FURNISHING SELF-ADMINISTERED HORMONAL CONTRACEPTIVES

A pharmacist can furnish <u>self-administered hormonal contraceptives</u>, which includes oral formulations (birth control <u>pills</u>), transdermal (the <u>patch</u>, such as *Xulane)*, vaginal (the <u>ring</u>, such as *NuvaRing)* and <u>injection</u> (such as *Depo-SubQ Provera 104).*[172]

Pharmacists who participate in this protocol must complete at least <u>one hour</u> of a board-approved CE program. The program must be specific to self-administered hormonal contraception, application of the <u>United States Medical Eligibility Criteria (USMEC)</u> for contraceptive use and other CDC guidance on contraception. An equivalent curriculum-based training program, completed on or after the year 2014 in an accredited California school of pharmacy, is also sufficient training to participate in this protocol.

The protocol requires that the pharmacist complete these steps:

- Ask the patient to complete the <u>self-screening form</u>; the form is based on the current USMEC, developed by the CDC.

  - The self-screening form should be available in languages commonly seen at the pharmacy.

  - The patient will need to complete the self-screening form <u>initially</u> and again <u>annually</u>, or whenever the patient indicates a <u>major health change</u>.

  - The form includes questions that can identify the use of drugs that could decrease contraceptive efficacy, such as drugs for epilepsy which are enzyme inducers.

  - The pharmacist reviews the answers and clarifies responses. The use of contraception <u>may be prohibited based on the responses</u>, such as having a history of breast cancer, heart disease, DVT or tobacco use.

  - If the pharmacist finds that it is not safe to provide the contraception or that the efficacy could be impaired, the patient should be referred to their PCP or to a nearby clinic for further assistance.

- Measure and record the patient's seated <u>blood pressure</u> if <u>combined (estrogen and progestin) hormonal contraceptives</u> are requested or recommended.

- Ensure that the patient is trained in administration and has received counseling on the product, including: (1) the dose, (2) the effectiveness, (3) potential side effects, (4) safety concerns, (5) the importance of receiving preventative health screenings, and (6) the lack of protection against sexually transmitted infections. The medication dispensed will be documented in the patient's profile.

---

172 CCR 1746.1

www.fda.gov/birthcontrol

BIRTH CONTROL GUIDE

If you do not want to get pregnant, there are many birth control options to choose from. No one product is best for everyone. Some methods are more effective than others at preventing pregnancy. Check the pregnancy rates on this chart to get an idea of how effective the product is at preventing pregnancy. The pregnancy rates tell you the number of pregnancies expected per 100 women during the first year of typical use. Typical use shows how effective the different methods are during actual use (including sometimes using a method in a way that is not correct or not consistent). The only sure way to avoid pregnancy is not to have any sexual contact. Talk to your healthcare provider about the best method for you.

FDA-Approved Methods	Number of pregnancies expected (per 100 Women)*	Use	Some Risks or Side Effects* This chart does not list all of the risks and side effects for each product.
Sterilization Surgery for Women	Less than 1	Onetime procedure. Permanent.	Pain Bleeding Infection or other complications after surgery
Sterilization Implant for Women	Less than 1	Onetime procedure. Permanent.	Pain/ cramping Pelvic or back discomfort Vaginal bleeding
Sterilization Surgery for Men	Less than 1	Onetime procedure. Permanent.	Pain Bleeding Infection
IUD Copper	Less than 1	Inserted by a healthcare provider. Lasts up to 10 years.	Cramps Heavier, longer periods Spotting between periods
IUD with Progestin	Less than 1	Inserted by a healthcare provider. Lasts up to 3-5 years, depending on the type.	Irregular bleeding No periods (amenorrhea) Abdominal/pelvic pain
Implantable Rod	Less than 1	Inserted by a healthcare provider. Lasts up to 3 years.	Menstrual Changes Mood swings or depressed mood Weight gain Headache Acne
Shot/ Injection	6	Need a shot every 3 months.	Loss of bone density Irregular bleeding/ Bleeding between periods Headaches Weight gain Nervousness Dizziness Abdominal discomfort
Oral Contraceptives "The Pill" (Combined Pill)	9	Must swallow a pill every day.	Spotting/ bleeding between periods Nausea Breast tenderness Headache
Oral Contraceptives "The Pill" (Extended/ Continuous Use Combined Pill)	9	Must swallow a pill every day.	Spotting/ bleeding between periods Nausea Breast tenderness Headache
Oral Contraceptives "The Mini Pill" (Progestin Only)	9	Must swallow a pill at the same time every day.	Spotting/ bleeding between periods Nausea Breast tenderness Headache
Patch	9	Put on a new patch each week for 3 weeks (21 total days). Don't put on a patch during the fourth week.	Spotting or bleeding between menstrual periods Nausea Stomach pain Breast tenderness Headache Skin irritation
Vaginal Contraceptive Ring	9	Put the ring into the vagina yourself. Keep the ring in your vagina for 3 weeks and then take it out for one week.	Vaginal discharge, discomfort in the vagina, and mild irritation. Headache Mood changes Nausea Breast tenderness
Diaphragm with Spermicide	12	Must use every time you have sex.	Irritation Allergic reactions Urinary tract infection
Sponge with Spermicide	12-24	Must use every time you have sex.	Irritation
Cervical Cap with Spermicide	17-23	Must use every time you have sex.	Irritation Allergic reactions Abnormal Pap test
Male Condom	18	Must use every time you have sex. Provides protection against some STDs.	Irritation Allergic reactions
Female Condom	21	Must use every time you have sex. Provides protection against some STDs.	Discomfort or pain during insertion or sex. Burning sensation, rash or itching
Spermicide Alone	28	Must use every time you have sex.	Irritation Allergic reactions Urinary tract infection

Most Effective ↑ Least Effective

OTHER CONTRACEPTION

Emergency Contraceptives (EC):

May be used if you did not use birth control or if your regular birth control fails (such as a condom breaks). It should not be used as a regular form of birth control. Emergency contraception prevents about 55 - 85% of predicted pregnancies.

Levonorgestrel 1.5 mg (1 pill) Levonorgestrel .75 mg (2 pills)	7 out of every 8 women who would have gotten pregnant will not become pregnant after taking this EC.	Swallow the pills as soon as possible within 3 days after having unprotected sex.	Menstrual changes Headache Nausea Dizziness Vomiting Breast pain Tiredness Lower stomach (abdominal) pain
Ulipristal Acetate	6 or 7 out of every 10 women who would have gotten pregnant will not become pregnant after taking this EC.	Swallow the pills within 5 days after having unprotected sex.	Headache Nausea Abdominal pain Menstrual pain Tiredness Dizziness

*For more information on the chance of getting pregnant while using a method or on the risks of a specific product, please check the product label or Trussell, J. (2011). "Contraceptive failure in the United States." Contraception 83(5):397-404.

Source: Food and Drug Administration

- Provide the patient with three Fact Sheets: (1) a birth control guide such as the one from the FDA (see previous page),[173] (2) the <u>patient package insert</u> (PPI), and (3) an administration Fact Sheet for the specific formulation.

- Refer all patients to their PCP or to a nearby clinic for follow-up. Notify the patient's PCP of any drugs or devices furnished. If the patient does not have a PCP, the pharmacist must provide the patient with a written record of drugs/devices provided.

- If self-administered hormonal contraception services are not immediately available or the pharmacist declines to provide them based on a conscience clause, the pharmacist must refer the patient to another pharmacist or facility to get the product the patient has requested.

- State mandatory reporting laws (discussed further) must be followed if sexual abuse is suspected.

- Keep records for <u>three years</u>.

FURNISHING TRAVEL MEDICATIONS

A pharmacist can furnish travel medications that do not require a diagnosis. This covers medications for travel <u>outside of the United States</u>. The prescription drug must be for either a condition that is both self-diagnosable and self-treatable, according to the CDC, or for prophylaxis.[174] Examples of these conditions and some of their treatment options are provided in the Study Tip below.[175]

SELECT SELF-DIAGNOSABLE CONDITIONS AND TREATMENT OPTIONS

Pharmacists can provide individuals traveling out of the United States with medication for self-treatment while they are away. The following are examples of conditions and medications that can be used for their treatment.

Motion Sickness: prochlorperazine, scopolamine

Travelers' Diarrhea: azithromycin, ciprofloxacin, rifaximin

Urinary Tract Infection (UTI): nitrofurantoin, sulfamethoxazole/trimethoprim

Vaginal Candidiasis: fluconazole

In order to furnish travel medications, the pharmacist must meet the following requirements:

- Complete an approved <u>immunization certificate program</u>

- Complete an approved <u>travel medicine training program</u>, which must consist of at least <u>10 hours</u> and cover each element of *The International Society of Travel Medicine's Body of Knowledge for the Practice of Travel Medicine (2012)*

- Complete the CDC's *Yellow Fever Vaccine Course*

- Have current <u>basic life support certification</u>

- Complete <u>two hours of CE</u> focused on travel medicine (separate from CE on immunizations and vaccines) <u>every two years</u>

---

173   https://www.fda.gov/media/135111/download (accessed 2020 Nov 13)
174   B&PC 4052(a)(10)(A)(3)
175   https://wwwnc.cdc.gov/travel/yellowbook/2020/preparing-international-travelers/the-pretravel-consultation (accessed 2020 Nov 13)

The pharmacist must follow these steps to furnish travel medications:

- Provide a "good faith evaluation" and assess the travel needs according to the patient's health status and the destinations they will visit. The travel history must include all the information necessary for a risk assessment during a pre-travel consultation; this is outlined in the CDC's *Yellow Book*.[176]

- Notify the patient's PCP of the drugs dispensed within 14 days of furnishing, or enter the information in a shared record system, or provide the patient with a written record of the drugs received to provide to a PCP of their choice.

- Provide the patient with a written record of the drugs provided.

FURNISHING PRE-EXPOSURE PROPHYLAXIS (PrEP)

Pre-exposure prophylaxis (PrEP) is a method for preventing HIV in which people who do not have HIV receive antiretroviral medications to reduce their risk of becoming infected. PrEP is recommended for individuals who are at very high risk for sexual exposure to HIV (e.g., the spouse is HIV positive) as well as for active intravenous drug users. Before furnishing PrEP, the pharmacist must complete a board-approved training program.

Pharmacists can furnish at least a 30-day supply (up to a 60-day supply) of tenofovir disoproxil fumarate (TDF) 300 mg / emtricitabine (FTC) 200 mg once daily *(Truvada)* to patients who meet the following criteria:

- A negative HIV test within the last 7 days using an HIV antigen/antibody test, antibody-only test or rapid point-of-care fingerstick blood test. If recent HIV results are not available, the pharmacist must order an HIV test and ensure a negative result before furnishing PrEP.

  - All positive HIV tests should be referred to a primary care provider.

- No signs or symptoms of acute HIV infection (e.g., fever, fatigue, sore throat, rash).

- Does not take any medications that are contraindicated with the PrEP regimen.

The pharmacist must provide counseling, which cannot be waived by the patient. The pharmacist may educate about:

- Side effects
- Safety during pregnancy and breastfeeding
- Adherence to the regimen
- Importance of timely testing and treatment

The pharmacist must notify the patient that all future prescriptions for PrEP must be supplied by a primary care provider. The pharmacist can furnish a maximum of 60 days of PrEP to a single patient over a two-year period. The services provided by the pharmacist must be documented in the patient record and the primary care provider must be notified. If the patient does not have a primary care provider or the patient refuses consent, the patient must be provided with a list of healthcare providers that can be contacted for follow-up care.

---

176   http://www.pharmacy.ca.gov/publications/travel_health_history_form.pdf (accessed 2020 Nov 13)

FURNISHING POST-EXPOSURE PROPHYLAXIS (PEP)

Post-exposure prophylaxis (PEP) is the use of antiretroviral drugs after a single exposure to HIV in order to prevent transmission. Exposure to HIV can be either occupational (occurring at work) or nonoccupational. Occupational exposure typically refers to exposure of healthcare personnel to blood or bodily fluids that are potentially contaminated with HIV. Nonoccupational exposure most commonly occurs from unprotected sex or intravenous drug use. PEP should be started as soon as possible after the exposure, ideally within 72 hours. Before furnishing PEP, the pharmacist must complete a board-approved training program.

Pharmacists can furnish a complete course of treatment (28 days) with one of the following PEP regimens to a patient who reports an exposure within the past 72 hours:

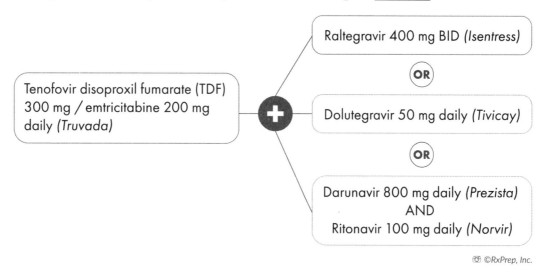

©RxPrep, Inc.

The pharmacist must offer HIV testing to the patient. If the patient refuses an HIV test, the pharmacist may still furnish PEP. The pharmacist must provide counseling, which cannot be waived by the patient. The counseling may include the same content as listed for PrEP.

For patients who are at high risk of developing HIV, the pharmacist must educate about the option of using a PrEP regimen for prevention. The services provided by the pharmacist must be documented in the patient record and the primary care provider must be notified. If the patient does not have a primary care provider or the patient refuses consent, the patient must be provided with a list of heathcare providers that can be contacted for follow-up care.

PROVIDING CLINICAL SERVICES

CLIA-WAIVED TESTS

A pharmacist can perform blood glucose, hemoglobin A1C (referred to as A1C), cholesterol, and PT/INR tests that are waived under the Clinical Laboratory Improvement Amendments (CLIA); no California Department of Public Health (CDPH) registration is required. All other CLIA-waived clinical laboratory tests require CDPH registration.

PHYSICAL ASSESSMENTS

Healthcare provider status broadens pharmacists' scope of practice as members of the interdisciplinary healthcare team in all settings. This enables pharmacists to perform physical assessments as part of an initial patient interview or to monitor drug treatment. See the RxPrep NAPLEX Course Book chapter on Answering Case-Based Exam Questions for further discussion.

Documentation is <u>required</u> for patient assessment, including results from the initial interview, monitoring appointments and referrals. Adequate documentation improves the quality of care and permits appropriate continuity of care.

PHYSICAL ASSESSMENT

Conduct Patient Interview

The physical assessment begins with an interview in a space that protects <u>patient privacy</u> and makes the patient feel comfortable. To establish rapport, the pharmacist should greet the patient by name, properly introduce themself and explain their role and the purpose of the visit.

Questions should be <u>open-ended</u> unless a simple factual response is needed. Open-ended questions require the patient to actually describe their complaints, giving much more accurate, patient-specific information than closed-ended questions. An open-ended question can begin with *"Tell me about...,"* *"Describe for me...,"* or *"Explain to me..."* An example of an open-ended question for a patient complaining of dizziness is *"What were you doing before you became dizzy?"*

<u>Closed-ended</u> questions are answered with a <u>simple, one-word response</u>. An example of a closed-ended question would be *"Do you feel dizzy when you first get out of bed in the morning or if you stand up suddenly?"* The patient would answer with a "yes" or "no." Closed-ended questions can be appropriate when confirming information.

ⓒ ESB Basic/Shutterstock.com

Active listening is required for a successful interview. Listening carefully to the patient conveys compassion and provides more insightful responses. Simple acknowledgements to demonstrate listening or understanding can be useful, such as *"I can see that"* or *"I understand why you that makes you feel anxious."* Avoid writing down notes or typing while the patient is speaking since this can be interpreted as a lack of complete attention. Observe the patient's body language and physical appearance to assess if the patient seems well, or appears energetic, tired or anxious.

Obtain Health History, with Medication Use

The health history includes the chief complaint (CC), the history of present illness (HPI), the past medical history (PMH), the social history, the family history (first-degree relatives), allergies, intolerances and reactions and medication use. The social history should include alcohol, tobacco and illicit (recreational) drug use. The medication use should include OTC medications and dietary or other supplements.

If the patient is a current tobacco user and is willing to try tobacco cessation, the pharmacist should counsel using the 5 A's Model (Ask, Advise, Assess, Assist and Arrange). Counseling and medication use should be recommended in combination. Both approaches, when used together, achieve higher quit rates.

Vital Sign Measurement: Blood Pressure, Heart Rate, Respiratory Rate, Temperature (and Pain)

Vital signs (blood pressure, heart rate, respiratory rate and temperature) are measurements of the human body's most basic functions and are useful in detecting and monitoring medical problems. The Joint Commission requires that pain be assessed and managed in all Joint Commission-accredited facilities, which includes many hospitals.

PHYSICAL ASSESSMENT

Blood Pressure

Blood pressure (BP) that remains high for an extended period of time (hypertension) can lead to severe consequences, including heart failure, stroke and kidney failure. Low BP (hypotension) may not be a serious issue as long as the patient feels fine. However, orthostatic hypotension (e.g., a sudden drop in BP when standing up from sitting or lying down) is dangerous because of the subsequent dizziness and risk of falls. Sudden drops in BP due to low or high body temperature, infection, dehydration, bleeding or an allergic reaction are serious. Patients who are found to have BP outside of the normal range at a healthcare screening should be referred for medical care. See the Hypertension and Acute & Critical Care Medicine chapters in the RxPrep NAPLEX Course Book for further discussion on treatment.

To measure BP accurately:

® Photographee.eu/Shutterstock.com

- Ask about recent tobacco, alcohol and caffeine, which can increase BP. Advise patients not to smoke tobacco or drink alcohol/caffeine at least 30 minutes before having BP taken.

- BP should be measured after the patient has used the restroom to empty their bladder, and has rested comfortably for five minutes in a chair that supports the back, with the feet resting on the floor.

- Instruct the patient to sit and refrain from talking during the measurement. Do not measure over clothing that constricts the arm.

- The arm being measured should be resting on a table or armchair at the same level as the heart.

- Use a sphygmomanometer with a stethoscope or an electronic BP machine with an appropriate size cuff.

- At the initial visit, take two readings (one in each arm), 1-2 minutes apart and record the average. At subsequent visits measure the arm with the higher pressure.

- In elderly patients, or if dizziness or lightheadedness is present, measure for orthostatic hypotension while the patient is standing. Take the standing measurement 1-2 minutes after the sitting measurement. Orthostatic hypotension is present if the SBP decreases at least 20 mmHg or if the DBP decreases at least 10 mmHg.

Sphygmomanometer technique:

- Select the proper size cuff.

- Wrap the cuff snugly around the arm with the marker on the cuff placed over the brachial artery. The lower part of the cuff should be above the elbow. Two fingers should fit snugly under the cuff.

- Place diaphragm or bell of stethoscope over the brachial artery and under the cuff.

- Pump the bulb until pressure is 30 mmHg above the estimated SBP.

- Slowly open the valve to allow the pressure to fall while listening for the Korotkoff sounds (sound of blood flowing).

- The SBP is when the Korotkoff sounds first appear. If this is missed, begin again with a higher initial pressure.

- The DBP is when the Korotkoff sounds disappear.

- When finished, rapidly release the remaining pressure and remove the cuff.

PHYSICAL ASSESSMENT

Heart Rate

A normal resting heart rate (HR) for adults is between <u>60-100 beats per minute</u> (BPM). A fast HR (tachycardia) can be due to hypoglycemia, infection, dehydration, anxiety, pain, hyperthyroidism, anemia, arrhythmia, shock, excessive caffeine intake or drug use.

Drugs that commonly cause tachycardia include stimulants (of all types, including weight loss and ADHD drugs), decongestants (oral, and nasal with > 3 days use), beta-agonist over-use (such as albuterol), bupropion, antipsychotics and theophylline, especially with toxicity. Any type of extreme emotional or physical stress, including benzodiazepine and opioid withdrawal, will cause tachycardia.

🔲 Dragon Images/Shutterstock.com

Reflex tachycardia can be due to a decrease (or displacement) in blood volume, which causes the heart to compensate by increasing HR to maintain cardiac output. This can occur with the use of hydralazine, nitrates and the dihydropyridine (DHP) calcium channel blockers that have a strong vasodilation effect, such as nifedipine IR.

A low HR (bradycardia) may be normal for people who are athletes or those who exercise frequently, or can be due to an arrhythmia, organophosphate poisoning (such as from pesticides), hyperkalemia, hypothyroidism or may be drug-induced. A higher drug level will correlate with a higher degree of bradycardia, which could be a sign of overdose.

Drugs that can cause a low HR include beta-blockers, non-DHP calcium channel blockers, clonidine, digoxin, antiarrhythmics, including sotalol, amiodarone and dronedarone, the acetylcholinesterase inhibitors used for dementia such as donepezil, and guanfacine, including the ADHD formulation *Intuniv*. The initiation of fingolimod *(Gilenya)* for multiple sclerosis requires first-dose monitoring for bradycardia. The bradycardia from fingolimod is transient and only occurs when the drug is started or restarted.

To measure HR, place your index and middle fingers on the patient's <u>radial artery</u> (found on the inside of the wrist, just below the thumb) to feel the radial pulse. Count the pulse for 30 seconds and double the number to determine the beats per minute.

Respiratory Rate

A normal respiratory rate (RR) for adults is <u>12-20 breaths per minute</u>. Respiration rates can increase with asthma, COPD, anxiety, stress, heart failure, pneumonia, sepsis, ketoacidosis or stimulant drug use. A low respiratory rate can be due to opioids or hypothyroidism.

Respiratory rate can be measured by <u>watching and counting</u> the number of times the patient's <u>chest rises and falls</u> for 30 seconds, and doubling the result to determine the breaths per minute.

Temperature

Normal body temperature in a healthy adult can range from 97.8°F (36.5°C) to 99°F (37.2°C). High temperature (hyperthermia) can be caused by infection, trauma, cancer, blood disorders, immune disorders or drugs. Low temperature (hypothermia) can be caused by exposure to cold, excessive alcohol intake, hypothyroidism or hypoglycemia.

Temperature is usually determined by ear (tympanic) or mouth (oral) measurements. Rectal measurement is an alternative, but uncomfortable in most cases, and impractical in the pharmacy setting.

- <u>Tympanic</u> membrane temperatures are quick, safe and reliable. Make sure the ear canal is clear of earwax before aiming the beam of the thermometer at the tympanic membrane. Wait 2-3 seconds until the temperature reading appears.

- <u>Oral</u> temperatures are preferred over <u>rectal</u> but are not recommended when patients are restless or unable to close their mouths. If using an electronic thermometer, place the disposable cover over the probe and insert the thermometer under the patient's tongue. Ask the patient to close both lips. A temperature reading usually takes about 10 seconds.

PHYSICAL ASSESSMENT

Pain

Pain is subjective, and thus, the primary measurement for assessing pain is the <u>patient's own report</u>, along with <u>behavioral observations</u>. The patient should be asked to identify the onset and temporal pattern, the location, the description (using the patient's own words), the intensity (using a pain scale) and any aggravating or relieving factors. The pharmacist should record previous treatments and their effectiveness.

0 Pain Free	1 Very Mild	2 Discomforting	3 Tolerable	4 Distressing	5 Very Distressing	6 Intense	7 Very Intense	8 Utterly Horrible	9 Excruciating Unbearable	10 Unimaginable Unspeakable

Vectoral/Shutterstock.com

Pain assessment requires an adequate "psycho-social" evaluation, which includes an interview and assessment of the factors which could be contributing to the pain response. It is common for patients with chronic pain to have concurrent psychological and social concerns.

Findings from the physical assessment, and any neurological and diagnostic procedure results, should be included.

The Wong-Baker FACES Pain Rating Scale (shown) is a common tool for patients to communicate their pain level, or a temperature scale (from green for no pain to red for the worst pain) or a simple numeric scale can be used. See the Pain chapter of the RxPrep NAPLEX Course Book.

The Physical Exam

Hand washing is required before and after any patient interview or physical exam. It is best to wash hands and don gloves in front of the patient.

Physical examinations involve inspection, palpation, percussion and auscultation:

- Inspection is using visual observation to note any deformities or abnormalities in the patient's physical appearance.
- Palpation is using the hands to examine the patient's body, such as palpating the upper right quadrant of the abdomen to assess the liver for size, tenderness and masses.
- Percussion is tapping the fingers on the patient's body and listening to the sound produced to determine if the tissue is air-filled (tympanic, drum-like sound), fluid-filled (dull sound) or solid (dull sound). For example, dull sounds can indicate a solid mass such as a healthy liver or the presence of ascites.
- Auscultation is listening to the internal sounds of the patient's body (commonly the heart, lung or bowel sounds), usually with a stethoscope.

HEALTH SCREENINGS

The community pharmacy setting reaches more people than can be seen in medical offices and provides an opportunity to screen patients for health conditions. In addition to the community setting, some institutional pharmacies provide health screenings and other clinical services. Assessment of body fat, blood pressure, cholesterol, blood glucose, tobacco use, bone density and depression are performed through health screenings at California pharmacies. If results from the health screenings are abnormal, the patient can be offered services or, if needed, referred for further medical evaluation.

HEALTH SCREENINGS

Body Fat Analysis (BMI and Waist Circumference)

Being overweight or obese is a health problem associated with increased morbidity and mortality. Body mass index (BMI) is based on height and weight; review the BMI calculations and classifications in the RxPrep NAPLEX Course Book chapter Calculations IV: Clinical. A normal BMI is 18.5-24.9 kg/m². Waist circumference is used with BMI. If most of the fat is around the waist, there is high risk, which is defined for adults as a waist size > 40 inches for males or > 35 inches for females.

Blood Pressure Screening

Measurement and assessment of blood pressure is described in the Physical Assessment section.

Glucose Screening

The ADA guidelines recommend testing for diabetes and prediabetes using A1C, fasting plasma glucose (FPG) or two-hour plasma glucose after a 75 gram oral glucose load, known as an oral glucose tolerance test (OGTT). Using an OGTT is not practical in a community pharmacy setting. FPG testing is less expensive and can be used, but it requires the patient to fast for at least eight hours for accurate results. Patients at health screenings are generally not fasting. A1C testing does not require fasting, and provides an accurate long-term blood glucose reading, but is more expensive.

Screening can be offered to all adults age 45 years and older, and in adults of any age who are overweight or obese (BMI ≥ 25 for the general population or ≥ 23 in Asian Americans) with ≥ 1 risk factor. The pharmacist should review the patient's medications for any that can contribute to hyperglycemia. For more information regarding risk factors, please see the Diabetes chapter in the RxPrep NAPLEX Course Book.

Glucose screening technique:

- Always wear gloves when working with blood or body fluid samples; change gloves between each patient
- Insert a test strip into glucose meter
- Calibrate the glucose meter with control solution if necessary
- Have the patient warm up their hands; let the arm hang down at the person's side briefly to allow blood flow to the fingertips
- Have the patient wash their hands with warm soapy water or wipe their fingertip with an alcohol swab and let dry
- Prick the side of the fingertip (or alternate testing site, depending on the meter used) with a lancet
- Squeeze the fingertip to aid blood flow, if needed
- Touch one edge of the test strip to the drop of blood, drawing the blood sample into the test strip
- Have the patient apply pressure to the puncture site until bleeding stops
- Apply a bandage to the puncture site
- Record glucose reading
- Dispose of used supplies properly; lancets should be placed into a sharps container

HEALTH SCREENINGS

Cholesterol Screening

Cholesterol screenings are available at most community pharmacies. *CardioChek* is a cholesterol measuring device that meets the National Cholesterol Education Program (NCEP) standards for accuracy, and is a small, hand-held device. See the Dyslipidemia chapter in the RxPrep NAPLEX Course Book for cholesterol value interpretation.

Cholesterol screening technique using *CardioChek*:

- Always wear gloves when working with blood or body fluid samples; change gloves between each patient
- Insert the code chip that matches the lot of the test strips
- Insert test strip (avoid touching sample site)
- Have the patient warm up their hands; let the arm hang down at the person's side briefly to allow blood flow to the fingertips
- Have the patient wash their hands with warm soapy water or wipe their fingertip with an alcohol swab and let dry
- Prick the side of the fingertip with a lancet
- Squeeze the fingertip to aid blood flow, if needed
- Wipe away the first drop of blood with gauze and use the second blood drop for testing
- Touch end of capillary tube/pipette to the second drop of blood
- To avoid gaps and air bubbles in the capillary tube/pipette, position the capillary tube/pipette so it is slightly tilted upward
- Repeat as needed to fill the capillary tube/pipette with blood (cholesterol screening requires a larger blood sample volume compared to glucose screening)
- Insert plunger into capillary tube (no assembly needed for a capillary pipette)
- Place capillary tube with the inserted plunger (or capillary pipette) over test strip blood application window
- Hold the capillary tube/pipette slightly above the blood application window, making sure to avoid touching the surface of the strip
- Gently press the plunger down (or gently squeeze the bulb of the capillary pipette) to move the blood onto the test strip
- Have the patient apply pressure to the puncture site until bleeding stops; apply a bandage to the puncture site
- Results appear in approximately two minutes; record cholesterol reading
- Dispose of used supplies properly; lancets should be placed into a sharps container

Bone Density Screening

Pharmacies can offer bone density screenings with an <u>ultrasound densitometer</u> that measures the bone density in the heel. The densitometer is portable, quick, lacks X-ray emission and provides the T-score. The gold standard for measuring bone density is the <u>dual-energy X-ray absorptiometry (DXA) scan</u>. Since the DXA scan emits radiation and is large, it is not practical to use a DXA scan in the pharmacy setting. If it is determined that the patient has low bone density using an ultrasound densitometer, the patient should be referred for a physician consult and a DXA scan. Diagnostic criteria are discussed in the Osteoporosis, Menopause & Testosterone Use chapter of the RxPrep NAPLEX Course Book.

Screening for osteoporosis can be performed with an ultrasound densitometer following these steps:

- Have patient sit down and remove shoe and sock from the foot that will be tested
- Apply gel to machine and bare heel, if necessary
- Place patient's heel in machine
- Membranes will fill with warm water and surround heel and ankle
- Results appear in approximately one minute; record reading
- Wipe off excess gel and clean membranes

HEALTH SCREENINGS

Depression Screening

The incidence of adult depression is between 3-5%. Increasingly, pharmacists are adding depression screening to medication therapy management (MTM) reviews. Screening for depression consists of asking the patient a series of questions, which is then scored.

Patients at risk for depression include those with substance abuse, other mental health conditions, pain, cancer or heart disease. In the elderly, long-term health changes that impair functional level increases the risk for depression, as does loneliness, grief and insomnia. Women who are pregnant or postpartum are at risk for depression and should be screened. Women and younger adults have higher risk.

There are several recommended screening forms that have been well-validated and which vary based on patient group.[177] The one used commonly for adults, the Patient Health Questionnaire (PHQ-9) is a simple check-off form that correlates to a score that indicates depression risk.[178]

Tobacco Screening

Screening for tobacco use should be done routinely and should be part of a more comprehensive MTM review. This practice will identify many smokers; 16.8% of the adult population in the U.S. smokes cigarettes. Tobacco cessation and furnishing NRT to patients was discussed previously.

QUALITY ASSURANCE PROGRAMS

NATIONAL PATIENT SAFETY GOALS

The purpose of The Joint Commission's National Patient Safety Goals (NPSGs) is to foster improvements in patient safety in Joint Commission-accredited facilities. The NPSGs highlight problematic areas in healthcare (such as the lack of consistently following CDC hand hygiene recommendations, or harm from the improper use of anticoagulants). Each NPSG targets one area and recommends steps to improve safety and reduce risk. Refer to the Medication Safety & Quality Improvement chapter of the RxPrep NAPLEX Course Book for further discussion.

STANDARD ORDER SETS

The use of standard order sets can promote best practice, decrease medication errors, improve workflow, improve patient outcomes and standardize patient care.[179] Standard order sets reduce the need to call prescribers for clarification about an order.

Standard order sets provide a benefit only when they are carefully developed and implemented at the facility. Standard order sets should be evidence-based and should not include non-formulary medications, drugs withdrawn from the market or equipment no longer available at the facility. Baseline tests, monitoring frequency and when emergency treatment (e.g., the use of reversal agents with anticoagulants) is required should be included in the order set. The table on the following page shows part of a standard order set for administering potassium to treat hypokalemia. Note that additional steps, such as follow-up lab draws, would be required and included in the full order set.

---

177   Effective depression screening tests in addition to PHQ-9 include the Hospital Anxiety and Depression Scales (for adults, inpatient), the Geriatric Depression Scale (for older adults), and the Edinburgh Postnatal Depression Scale (for postpartum and pregnant women).

178   https://www.drugabuse.gov/sites/default/files/PatientHealthQuestionnaire9.pdf (accessed 2020 Nov 13)

179   http://www.ismp.org/tools/guidelines/standardordersets.pdf (accessed 2020 Nov 13)

SERUM POTASSIUM (MEQ/L)	INSTRUCTION
< 2.6	100 mEq KCl IV; contact MD
2.6 – 2.9	80 mEq KCl IV; contact MD
3.0 – 3.2	60 mEq KCl IV
3.3 – 3.5	40 mEq KCl IV

ANTIMICROBIAL STEWARDSHIP PROGRAMS

Antimicrobials (e.g., antibiotics) are often overused/misused despite the risk of potentially serious side effects. The misuse of antibiotics contributes to the spread of antibiotic resistance and the creation of multidrug-resistant organisms (sometimes referred to as "superbugs"). Superbugs are strains of bacteria that are resistant to several types of antibiotics. Some of these resistant pathogens are untreatable with the antibiotics available today.

Antimicrobial Stewardship Programs (ASPs) ensure that hospitalized patients receive the right antibiotic, at the right dose, at the right time and for the right duration.[180] Culture and susceptibility data can be used to select the antibiotic with the narrowest possible spectrum for continuation of therapy. Using antibiotics appropriately will reduce antibiotic resistance and the evolution of multidrug-resistant organisms. Please review the Infectious Diseases chapters in the RxPrep NAPLEX Course Book for the appropriate use of antibiotics.

MEDICATION UTILIZATION EVALUATIONS

The American Society of Health-System Pharmacists (ASHP) defines a medication-use evaluation (MUE) as a "performance improvement method that focuses on evaluating and improving medication-use processes with the goal of optimal patient outcomes."[181] In other words, it is a process to improve the use of drugs to increase the health benefit for patients. MUEs are often conducted in individual institutions and sometimes as part of a larger effort to improve care across healthcare systems. MUEs can be conducted for a specific drug (e.g., morphine), drug class (e.g., opioids), disease state (e.g., pain) or a process (such as prescribing, dispensing or administration).

An MUE can be interdisciplinary (involve the nurses, physicians, pharmacists, and others) in order to achieve the best results and implement the recommendations. It is important to identify ways to use the drugs safely and ensure that the facility follows the recommendations. The MUE process involves collecting and analyzing the events, improving software to avoid future events and developing an action plan, which can include a standard order set and treatment pathway.

An MUE can be used when a drug is especially toxic, when it is used in a group at high risk of adverse drug reactions (ADRs), when a medication is being considered for addition to or removal from the formulary or to identify poor and/or costly prescribing habits. The purposes for MUEs include: determining optimal medication therapy, preventing medication-related problems, evaluating the efficacy of a medication and improving patient safety.

---

180   http://www.cdc.gov/getsmart/healthcare/evidence.html (accessed 2020 Nov 13)
181   https://www.ashp.org/-/media/assets/policy-guidelines/docs/guidelines/medication-use-evaluation.ashx (accessed 2020 Nov 13)

PEER REVIEW AND SELF-EVALUATION

A performance evaluation process conducted by peers and/or oneself is part of the quality assurance process. Evaluation can include standard objective criteria and position-specific criteria. Peer experts are commonly involved in establishing competencies required for granting privileges, such as granting some type of practice designation or the use of a high-risk agent. The standards involved with any type of privilege are continually updated as needed.

MEDICATION ERROR REPORTING

Although pharmacists practice with the best intentions, medication errors occur. The most common type of error in community pharmacy is dispensing the wrong medication to a patient. It is estimated that the overall dispensing accuracy rate in community pharmacy is 98.3%, which is approximately four errors per 250 prescriptions, according to the Institute for Safe Medication Practices (ISMP). California requires <u>all pharmacies to have a quality assurance (QA) program</u> to document, assess and prevent medication errors. There must be a readily-retrievable policy and procedure (P&P) for the QA program so the pharmacy staff knows what to do when a medication error occurs.

Investigation of pharmacy medication errors must begin <u>within two business days</u> from the date the medication error was discovered; otherwise, the sequence of events leading up to the event will be forgotten. The sooner the incident is documented, the better. Preferably, and especially if the consequences of the error are severe, the assessment should be conducted using a root cause analysis (RCA). An RCA is used to discover the causes in the system (i.e., the dispensing process) that led to the error and design changes to avoid making the same mistake. RCA is discussed in more detail in the Medication Safety & Quality Improvement chapter of the RxPrep NAPLEX Course Book. The record of the QA review should be immediately retrievable in the pharmacy (i.e., it cannot be stored off-site) and must be <u>kept in the pharmacy</u> for at least <u>one year</u> from the date it was created. The record must contain the following information[182]:

- Date, location and participants in the QA review
- Pertinent data related to the medication error
- Findings and determinations of factors that could have contributed to the error
- Recommended changes to pharmacy policy, procedure, systems or processes to avoid a repeat of the medication error

The pharmacist must <u>inform the patient</u> that a medication error has occurred and should inform the patient of any <u>steps that can be taken to avoid further injury</u> (such as the use of another agent to lessen the effects of a drug taken in error). The pharmacist must also <u>inform the prescriber</u> that a medication error has occurred.

182   CCR 1711

PROMOTING PUBLIC HEALTH

MEDICARE PART D

Medicare is a federal health insurance program for people ages ≥ 65 or < 65 with disability, and patients with end-stage renal disease (ESRD). Medicare Part D is the drug benefit for Medicare enrollees. Medicare enrollees can apply for a Low Income Subsidy (LIS), which pays for the Part D monthly premium, the annual deductible and medication copays.

In addition to federal Medicare, lower income children, pregnant women, families and low-income adults may qualify for state Medicaid. Enrollees in Medicaid do not have copays. In California, the state Medicaid is called Medi-Cal.

All Medicare recipients in California are able to obtain drugs at the Medi-Cal reimbursement rate. There are Medicare plans with prescription drug coverage, including many of the Medicare Advantage plans, which are offered by private companies as alternatives to traditional Medicare.

Medicare uses a Star Rating System (on a scale of 1 to 5 stars) to determine how well Medicare Advantage and Medicare Part D prescription drug plans perform. Plans with higher ratings get perks, such as an additional "special enrollment period" (versus once yearly enrollment).[183] Medicare Part D ratings are based on several quality measures and can change from year to year.[184] Examples of quality measures that may be included in the ratings related to drug therapy include[185]:

- Annual comprehensive medication review (CMR) for patients enrolled in an MTM program.
- Adherence to diabetes medications, statins and renin-angiotensin system antagonists (including ACE inhibitors, ARBs and aliskiren).
- Ensuring statin use in patients with diabetes age 40 to 75 years old.
- Appropriate use or avoidance of high-risk medications in patients 65 years and older.

183 https://www.medicare.gov/sign-up-change-plans/when-can-i-join-a-health-or-drug-plan/5-star-special-enrollment-period (accessed 2020 Nov 13)

184 https://www.medicareinteractive.org/get-answers/medicare-health-coverage-options/changing-medicare-coverage/how-to-compare-plans-using-the-medicare-star-rating-system#:~:text=Medicare%20uses%20a%20Star%20Rating,and%20one%20being%20the%20lowest. (accessed 2020 Nov 13)

185 https://www.pqaalliance.org/medicare-part-d (accessed 2020 Nov 13)

COVERED CALIFORNIA

Covered California is the name of the health insurance "marketplace" in California. This includes a website where patients can compare the different ACA plans and enroll for coverage. All of the plans offered through Covered California provide prescription drugs, which are included as one of the "essential health benefits" that the ACA plans must include, in addition to contraception, described previously, and other services.[186]

Covered California was launched in 2014. Covered California plans are sold in four levels of coverage: <u>Bronze, Silver, Gold and Platinum</u>. For patients under <u>30 years of age</u>, another option, called the <u>minimum coverage plan</u>, is also available. The higher-cost plans pay a higher percentage of covered medical expenses than what a patient would be expected to pay in copays and annual deductibles.

Patients should enroll in plans based on their individual health needs. A young, healthy person may choose to enroll in the minimum coverage plan or Bronze plan since this person only anticipates going to the doctor once a year for an annual check-up. A patient with several comorbidities, or who requires expensive specialty drugs and regular follow-up visits with a specialist, may find it more cost-effective to enroll in a Platinum plan. Even though the Platinum plan has a higher monthly premium, the co-pay for doctor visits and prescription drugs are lower than the Bronze plan.

PATIENT ASSISTANCE PROGRAMS

Patient assistance programs (PAPs) help <u>low-income, uninsured</u> patients get <u>free or low-cost, brand-name medications</u>. These programs are typically provided by the <u>drug manufacturer</u> that makes the drug. There are several online directories that help patients find a specific patient assistance program, including the popular RxAssist site at www.rxassist.org. See the example in the box below.

If the patient meets the requirements, they qualify to receive the drug at no cost.

Example Eligibility Information:

- Must not have prescription coverage and must not be eligible for state or federal programs such as Medicare and Medicaid.

- For most medications, patients with Medicare Part D might be considered if they are ineligible for Low Income Subsidy and have spent at least 5% of their annual household income (out-of-pocket) on medications.

- Patient must be under the care of a licensed healthcare provider who is authorized to prescribe, dispense, and administer medicine in the U.S.

- For vaccines, patient must be at least 19 years of age.

---

186   https://www.coveredca.com/individuals-and-families/getting-covered/coverage-basics/essential-health-benefits/ (accessed 2020 Nov 13)

TABLET SPLITTING

Splitting tablets can <u>save patients</u> and health plans <u>money</u> because manufacturers sometimes charge the same price for higher and lower doses of the same drug.

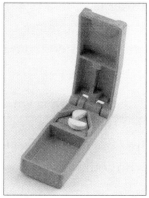

Raihana Asral/Shutterstock.com

The easiest tablets to split are the ones that are <u>scored</u>. Patients should use commercially available devices ("pill cutters" or "pill splitters") specifically designed to split tablets. Patients should not use a kitchen knife or other tools that can result in an uneven split or accidently hurt the patient. Split tablets can deteriorate and lose their effectiveness when exposed to air and moisture for too long, so splitting should occur close to the time the dose is needed.[187]

Not all drugs can be safely or practically split. There are some tablets that <u>crumble easily</u> and others that are <u>coated</u> to protect the GI lining or to prevent the drug from degrading in the stomach. Patients with <u>manual dexterity problems</u> (e.g., arthritis, Parkinson disease), <u>visual impairment</u>, or <u>cognitive impairment</u> are not good candidates for tablet splitting. Capsules should never be split. Tablets that should not be split include those that are:

- Very small in size
- Asymmetrical in shape
- Narrow therapeutic index drugs
- Enteric-coated, film-coated or extended-release[188]

There are no California laws or pharmacy regulations specifically forbidding tablet splitting. The pharmacist and patient should decide whether splitting tablets is appropriate.

OTHER DRUG COST-SAVING STRATEGIES

There are other ways a pharmacist can advise a patient to save money on drugs[189]:

- The same drug can be less expensive at a different pharmacy; it may be useful to do a cost comparison.
- Consider using the <u>generic</u> equivalent of a brand-name drug.
- Suggest to the prescriber a <u>therapeutically similar but less expensive drug</u>. Keep in mind that drugs in advertisements are new and generally more expensive than older alternatives.
- Consider purchasing a <u>greater day supply</u> (i.e., 90-day instead of 30-day) if the copay is the same.

187   http://www.pharmacy.ca.gov/publications/pill_splitting_brochure.pdf (accessed 2020 Nov 13)
188   http://www.pharmacy.ca.gov/publications/07_jul_script.pdf (accessed 2020 Nov 13)
189   https://www.healthline.com/health/how-to-save-money-on-prescriptions (accessed 2020 Nov 13)

Manufacturers Offering Discounts of a Branded Drug

Patients should not be swayed to purchase a branded drug, even with a discount, if a lower-cost generic equivalent is available and is covered by their insurance. In California, <u>manufacturers</u> are <u>prohibited</u> from offering drug <u>discounts</u> for the purpose of <u>pushing a more costly branded drug</u> on the patient.

The <u>exception</u> is when the manufacturer is able to <u>offer the drug</u> at a discounted price which is <u>less</u> than the cost of the <u>generic equivalent</u>. Manufacturers are <u>permitted</u> to <u>provide</u> the drug <u>free</u> of charge to certain patients, such as those who are able to demonstrate a low income and who could otherwise not afford the drug.[190]

Pharmacies Must Inform Consumers of Lower Costs of Covered Drugs

The consumer must be informed of the lower price of a covered medication, whether it is the retail price or the cost-sharing (co-pay) amount, unless the pharmacy automatically charges the lower amount.[191] The insurance plan cannot require the consumer to pay more than the pharmacy's retail price.[192] <u>Pharmacists</u> must <u>ensure</u> that the patient gets the <u>lowest price available</u>.

---

190   H&SC 132000
191   B&PC 4079.5(a)
192   H&SC 1342.71 (f)(3)

CONTROLLED SUBSTANCES PART 1:
THE CONTROLLED SUBSTANCES ACT

CHAPTER CONTENTS

Controlled Substance Schedules..**94**

Common Controlled Substances by Schedule...95

Schedule Changes 98

State-Specific Scheduling...98

Formulation-Specific Scheduling 98

Cannabidiols & Tetrahydrocannabinols...**99**

FDA-Approved Products 99

Regulation of Cannabis Products in California 100

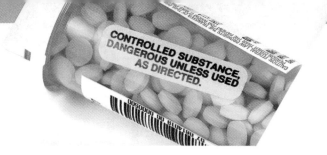

CHAPTER 5

CONTROLLED SUBSTANCES PART 1:
THE CONTROLLED SUBSTANCES ACT

CONTROLLED SUBSTANCE SCHEDULES

The Drug Enforcement Administration (DEA), under the U.S. Department of Justice (DOJ), enforces the requirements in the Controlled Substances Act (CSA). The DEA publishes the *Pharmacist's Manual,* which includes the details needed to comply with the CSA.[193]

The DEA determines which drugs should be classified as controlled substances and places them into one of five schedules (I – V). The schedule is determined based on whether the drug has a currently <u>accepted medical use</u>, its relative <u>abuse potential</u> and the potential for it to cause <u>dependence when abused</u>.

The <u>higher</u> the <u>abuse potential</u>, the <u>lower</u> the <u>schedule</u> number. <u>Schedule I</u> drugs have the <u>highest abuse potential</u> and are considered to have <u>no accepted medical use</u>. Drugs in this category (such as heroin and LSD) may be used for research purposes, but are most commonly used illicitly (illegally/unlawfully). Marijuana is an exception; it is classified as schedule I according to the DEA, but is available for medicinal and adult recreational use in California. <u>Schedule II – V</u> drugs are considered to have currently <u>accepted medical uses</u>, with varying degrees of abuse and dependence potential.

Recognizing common controlled substances by brand or generic name will be important on the exam. See the table starting on the following page for common drugs within each schedule.

CONTROLLED SUBSTANCE SCHEDULE DEFINITIONS

SCHEDULE	DEFINITION
I	No currently accepted medical use; high potential for abuse and lack of accepted safety under medical supervision.
II	High potential for abuse; abuse may cause severe psychological or physical dependence.
III	Lower abuse potential than schedules I and II; abuse may cause moderate or low potential for physical dependence or high psychological dependence.
IV	Low potential for abuse relative to schedule III; abuse may cause limited physical or psychological dependence relative to schedule III.
V	Low potential for abuse relative to schedule IV; abuse may cause limited physical or psychological dependence relative to schedule IV.

COMMON CONTROLLED SUBSTANCES BY SCHEDULE

SCHEDULE I

3,4-methylenedioxymethamphetamine or MDMA

Gamma-hydroxybutyric acid or GHB (the sodium salt form, sodium oxybate, is schedule III)

Heroin

Lysergic acid diethylamide or LSD

Marijuana (Cannabis sativa), per the DEA; legalized in some states

Mescaline

Peyote

SCHEDULE II	MUST KNOW BRAND NAMES	ADDITIONAL BRAND NAMES
Select Opioids		
Alfentanil		
Codeine, single ingredient		
Fentanyl	Actiq, Duragesic	Fentora, Lazanda, Sublimaze, Subsys
Hydrocodone, single ingredient	Hysingla ER, Zohydro ER	
Hydrocodone, combination products	Lortab, Norco, TussiCaps, Tussionex,* Vicodin,* Vicoprofen*	
Hydromorphone	Dilaudid	
Levorphanol		
Meperidine	Demerol*	
Methadone	Methadone HCl Intensol, Methadose	
Morphine	Kadian, MS Contin	Duramorph, Infumorph, Mitigo
Oxycodone, single ingredient	OxyContin, Roxicodone	Oxaydo, Xtampza ER
Oxycodone, combination products	Endocet, Percocet, Percodan	
Oxymorphone	Opana*	

SCHEDULE II	MUST KNOW BRAND NAMES	ADDITIONAL BRAND NAMES
Paregoric		
Sufentanil		
Tapentadol	Nucynta, Nucynta ER	
ADHD Stimulants		
Amphetamine		Adzenys ER, Adzenys ER-ODT, Dyanavel XR, Evekeo, Evekeo ODT
Amphetamine/Dextroamphetamine	Adderall,* Adderall XR	Mydayis
Dexmethylphenidate	Focalin, Focalin XR	
Dextroamphetamine	Dexedrine	
Lisdexamfetamine	Vyvanse	
Methamphetamine		Desoxyn
Methylphenidate	Concerta, Daytrana, Ritalin, Ritalin LA	Adhansia XR, Aptensio XR, Cotempla XR-ODT, Jornay PM, Metadate CD, Methylin, QuilliChew ER, Quillivant XR
Other		
Cocaine		
Dronabinol solution *Capsules (Marinol) are schedule III*	Syndros	
Levo-alpha-acetyl-methadol (LAAM)		
Pentobarbital		Nembutal
Secobarbital		Seconal

SCHEDULE III	MUST KNOW BRAND NAMES	ADDITIONAL BRAND NAMES
Benzphetamine		
Buprenorphine, single ingredient	Butrans	Belbuca, Buprenex, Probuphine, Sublocade
Buprenorphine/Naloxone	Suboxone	Zubsolv
Butabarbital		
Butalbital-containing products	Fioricet, Fioricet with Codeine, Fiorinal, Fiorinal with Codeine	Allzital, Bupap
Codeine/Acetaminophen	Tylenol with Codeine #3, Tylenol with Codeine #4	
Dronabinol capsules *Solution (Syndros) is schedule II*	Marinol	
Ketamine		Ketalar
Perampanel	Fycompa	
Phendimetrazine		
Sodium oxybate	Xyrem	
Testosterone and all anabolic steroids (look for "andro" in drug name, such as androstenedione)	Androderm, AndroGel	Aveed, Depo-Testosterone, Fortesta, Jatenzo, Natesto, Testim, Testopel, Vogelxo, Xyosted

SCHEDULE IV	MUST KNOW BRAND NAMES	ADDITIONAL BRAND NAMES
Benzodiazepines		
Alprazolam	Alprazolam Intensol, Xanax, Xanax XR	
Chlordiazepoxide	Librium	
Clobazam	Onfi	Sympazan
Clonazepam	Klonopin	
Clorazepate	Tranxene-T	
Diazepam	Diastat AcuDial, Diazepam Intensol, Valium	
Estazolam		
Flurazepam		
Lorazepam	Ativan, Lorazepam Intensol	
Midazolam	Versed	Nayzilam, Seizalam
Quazepam		Doral
Oxazepam		
Remimazolam	Byfavo	
Temazepam	Restoril	
Triazolam	Halcion	
Hypnotics		
Eszopiclone	Lunesta	
Lemborexant		DayVigo
Suvorexant		Belsomra
Zaleplon	Sonata	
Zolpidem	Ambien, Ambien CR, Edluar, Zolpimist	
Weight Loss Drugs		
Diethylpropion		
Phentermine	Adipex-P	Lomaira
Phentermine/Topiramate	Qsymia	
Other		
Armodafinil	Nuvigil	
Butorphanol	Stadol*	
Carisoprodol	Soma	
Difenoxin/Atropine		Motofen
Eluxadoline		Viberzi
Modafinil	Provigil	
Phenobarbital		
Tramadol	Ultram	ConZip
Tramadol/Acetaminophen	Ultracet	

SCHEDULE V	MUST KNOW BRAND NAMES	ADDITIONAL BRAND NAMES
Brivaracetam		*Briviact*
Codeine containing cough syrups (codeine/promethazine, codeine/promethazine/phenylephrine, codeine/guaifenesin, others)	*Cheratussin AC,* * *G Tussin AC, Robitussin A-C, Virtussin A/C*	
Diphenoxylate/atropine	*Lomotil*	
Lacosamide	*Vimpat*	
Pregabalin	*Lyrica, Lyrica CR*	

*Brand discontinued but name still used in practice.

SCHEDULE CHANGES

The DEA can reclassify a drug schedule when the perceived risk of abuse or dependence associated with the drug changes. When a scheduling change occurs, a pharmacy must complete an inventory of the drug on the date the change becomes effective. After the initial inventory, subsequent inventories are conducted according to the requirements of the new schedule.

STATE-SPECIFIC SCHEDULING

States can choose to classify drugs into stricter scheduling categories than the DEA. When state and federal pharmacy law differ, the stricter law should be followed. For example, *Fioricet* is not federally classified as a controlled substance, but California classifies *Fioricet* as schedule III.

FORMULATION-SPECIFIC SCHEDULING

Most controlled substances in the same pharmacological class or containing the same active ingredient will be classified in the same schedule (e.g., all benzodiazepines are schedule IV). Some controlled substances that are available as single-entity and combination products (e.g., oxycodone) are schedule II in all formulations due to the abuse potential. Other drugs (e.g., barbiturates, codeine and dronabinol) may have varying schedules based on the formulation.

Barbiturate Schedules

- Schedule II: single-entity oral formulations of amobarbital, pentobarbital and secobarbital
- Schedule III:
    - Amobarbital, pentobarbital and secobarbital formulated as a suppository
    - Amobarbital, pentobarbital and secobarbital in combination with a non-controlled substance
    - Butabarbital
    - Butalbital-containing products (*Fioricet, Fioricet with Codeine, Fiorinal, Fiorinal with Codeine*)
- Schedule IV: phenobarbital

Codeine Schedules

- Schedule II: <u>single-entity</u> products

- Schedule III: <u>combination tablets/capsules</u> that contain codeine [e.g., acetaminophen 300 mg/codeine 30 mg *(Tylenol #3)]*

- Schedule V: <u>combination cough syrups</u> that contain codeine (e.g., promethazine/phenylephrine HCl/codeine syrup)

Dronabinol Schedules

- Schedule II: <u>oral solution *(Syndros)*</u>, which is 50% alcohol

- Schedule III: <u>oral capsules *(Marinol)*</u>

CANNABIDIOLS & TETRAHYDROCANNABINOLS

Federal law designates marijuana as a schedule I controlled substance. <u>Cannabidiol (CBD)</u> and <u>tetrahydrocannabinol (THC)</u> are natural compounds found in the *Cannabis sativa* (marijuana) plant. <u>THC</u> has a <u>psychoactive effect</u> (a "high"). <u>CBD</u> does not cause a high, but can have an <u>anxiolytic (relaxing)</u> effect. <u>Hemp</u> is derived from a type of *Cannabis sativa* plant with levels of <u>THC (< 0.3%)</u> incapable of causing a psychoactive effect. Both THC and CBD are used for a variety of medical conditions, with and without proof of efficacy. The ratio of THC:CBD contributes to a product's therapeutic efficacy and psychoactive effect.

FDA-APPROVED PRODUCTS

Epidiolex (cannabidiol), the first FDA-approved <u>CBD-derived</u> product, is indicated for seizures associated with several disorders: Lennox-Gastaut syndrome, Dravet syndrome and tuberous sclerosis complex. Initially, the DEA placed *Epidiolex* in a new classification of schedule V that would include FDA-approved CBD drugs containing no more than 0.1% (w/w) residual THC. However, in 2020 the DEA descheduled *Epidiolex*, so it is now considered a <u>non-controlled</u> drug according to federal and California law.

There are also two FDA-approved <u>cannabis-related</u> drugs (i.e., not cannabis-derived, like *Epidiolex).*

- <u>Dronabinol</u>: a synthetic delta-9-tetrahydrocannabinol (synthetic THC) approved for AIDS-associated anorexia and chemotherapy-induced nausea and vomiting (CINV). It is available as an oral capsule *(<u>Marinol, schedule III</u>)* and an alcohol-containing oral solution *(<u>Syndros</u>, schedule II).*

- <u>Nabilone *(Cesamet*, schedule II)*</u>: a synthetic cannabinoid with a chemical structure similar to THC that is indicated for CINV.

*Brand discontinued but name still used in practice.

REGULATION OF CANNABIS PRODUCTS IN CALIFORNIA

In California, cannabis is regulated less stringently. Medical use of THC was decriminalized in California in 1996.[194] In 2014, non-medical use of cannabis and cannabis products (for adults) was permitted.[195] CBD and THC-containing products (including edibles) can be manufactured and sold. In states where recreational and medical marijuana is legal, such as California, CBD derived from the cannabis plant is taxed and regulated.

According to federal law, CBD derived from any source (including hemp) cannot be used in dietary supplements or as a food additive since CBD is available as a prescription drug *(Epidiolex)*. However, the DEA has made two recent changes pertaining to cannabis products:

- In 2018, the Farm Bill was signed into federal law, which removed hemp from the definition of marijuana in the CSA. Since hemp products are legal, CBD can be extracted from hemp and used in topical products (e.g., cream, oils, sprays).

- The FDA still regulates hemp and hemp-derived products, but they are no longer classified as schedule I. This has allowed retail pharmacies to begin selling CBD-containing topical products in select states, including California.

Currently, there is a proposed bill in California that would permit the sale of hemp-derived CBD in foods, beverages and cosmetics. The bill did not initially pass, but is scheduled to be reviewed again by the California legislature.

Since pharmacies are registered by the DEA, they must operate within the confines of the federal law regarding marijuana. As such, pharmacies are not permitted to sell marijuana or drug paraphernalia (e.g., rolling papers). Even though marijuana is not dispensed in pharmacies, pharmacists should add marijuana to a patient's medication profile, and be aware of potential drug interactions. CBD and THC are CNS depressants which can cause additive side effects. Both are also substrates of several CYP450 enzymes (i.e., inducers decrease and inhibitors increase CBD/THC levels).

194   1 7 USC 5940, subdiv. (b)(2)
195   H&SC 11362.1 (CA Proposition 64, passed and became effective in 2014)

CONTROLLED SUBSTANCES PART 2:
ORDERING AND DISPOSAL

CHAPTER CONTENTS

Ordering Controlled Substances **102**

Controlled Substance Registrants 102

Ordering Schedule III – V Drugs 103

Ordering Schedule I and II Drugs 103

DEA Form 222 104

Steps to Order Schedule II Drugs with Form 222 107

Electronic Controlled Substance Ordering System 108

Lost or Stolen DEA Form 222 or Electronic Orders 108

Distribution of Controlled Substances Between DEA Registrants 109

Cancelling or Voiding Controlled Substance Orders 110

Controlled Substance Loss or Theft 110

Disposal of Controlled Substances **112**

Registrants Returning Controlled Substances to the Supplier 112

Registrants Sending Controlled Substances to a Reverse Distributor 112

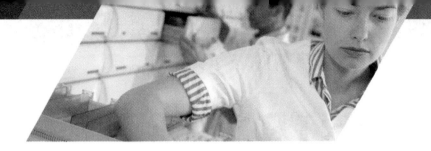

CONTROLLED SUBSTANCES PART 2:
ORDERING AND DISPOSAL

ORDERING CONTROLLED SUBSTANCES

Below are the DEA Forms related to managing controlled substances that should be known for the exam.

DEA FORMS FOR MANAGING CONTROLLED SUBSTANCES	

DEA FORM #	PURPOSE
224	Registration form for retail pharmacies, hospitals/clinics, teaching institutions, practitioners or mid-level practitioners
225	Registration form for drug manufacturers, distributors (e.g., supplier/wholesaler) and researchers
363	Registration form for narcotic (opioid) treatment clinics
510	Registration form for bulk chemical manufacturers and distributors
222	Ordering form for schedule I and II drugs
106	Reporting form for theft or significant loss of controlled substances
41	Record of controlled substances destroyed

CONTROLLED SUBSTANCE REGISTRANTS

Individual persons must register with the DEA for authorization to prescribe controlled substances. An exception is medical residents in a healthcare facility, who can prescribe controlled substances for patients within the institution by using the facility's DEA number. Facilities participating in the manufacture, distribution, research, prescribing and dispensing of controlled substances must also register with the DEA. The registration form used depends on the manner in which the applicant will manage controlled substances (see the Study Tip above). After approval of the registration, the DEA will assign the individual or facility a unique DEA number. This DEA number will allow a physician to prescribe controlled substances or authorize a pharmacy to order and dispense controlled substances.[196]

196 https://www.deadiversion.usdoj.gov/pubs/index.html (accessed 2020 Nov 13)

Healthcare providers practicing at the following facilities can <u>prescribe, administer or dispense</u> controlled substances <u>without registering with the DEA</u>:

- Federal Bureau of Prisons
- Indian Health Service
- U.S. Armed Forces (Air Force, Army, Coast Guard, Navy, Marine Corps, Space Force)
- U.S. Public Health Service

Providers that <u>purchase or procure</u> controlled substances (e.g., pharmacists) at these facilities are <u>not eligible</u> for this exemption and <u>must register</u> with the DEA.

ORDERING SCHEDULE III – V DRUGS

<u>Schedule III – V drugs</u> can be obtained from a supplier/wholesaler by using a <u>purchase order</u> or through the <u>Controlled Substance Ordering System</u> (CSOS). The invoice or a packing slip (e.g., receipt) is used to record the delivery date and to confirm that the correct items are received. The <u>receipts</u> must be readily available in the pharmacy and should <u>contain</u> the following information:

- <u>Name</u> of each controlled substance in the order
- Drug <u>formulation</u> (e.g., oral solution)
- <u>Number of dosage units</u> in each container
- <u>Number of packages</u> ordered and delivered

ORDERING SCHEDULE I AND II DRUGS

Before ordering schedule I or II drugs, the <u>pharmacist-in-charge</u> (i.e., registrant) must first <u>register</u> with the DEA <u>using Form 224</u>. CSOS can be used to order schedule I – V drugs, while DEA Form 222 is limited to obtaining schedule I and II drugs. Schedule I drugs have no currently accepted medical use, but they may be ordered for use in investigational research.

PAPER VERSUS ELECTRONIC ORDERING

	DEA FORM 222	CSOS
Method of submission	Paper	Electronic
Limit of items per order	10 items (triplicate form) 20 items (single-sheet form)	No limit
Drugs that can be ordered	Schedules I, II	Schedules I, II, III, IV, V
Typical turnaround time	2-5 business days	1-2 business days
Type of signature used	Handwritten signature	Digital signature
Can the order be endorsed to another supplier?*	Yes	No
When must the supplier report the transaction to the DEA?	By the end of the month during which the order was filled	Within 2 business days of filling the order

*If a supplier cannot fill all or part of the order, then the order can be endorsed to another supplier for filling. Only the initial supplier can endorse the order to another supplier.

The DEA registrant can request copies of Form 222 or CSOS access on the initial DEA Form 224 or through the DEA website. Each pharmacy location has <u>one designated registrant</u>. This is the only pharmacist authorized to order schedule I and II drugs, unless the registrant grants a <u>power of attorney</u> (POA) to another individual, allowing them to <u>place orders</u> for schedule I and II drugs in his/her absence. A <u>POA</u> is a legal document that <u>authorizes</u> a designated individual to <u>act in the registrant's place</u>.

The following provisions apply to the use of a POA:

- It can be granted to <u>licensed or unlicensed</u> pharmacy personnel.
- The registrant can grant <u>multiple POAs</u>.
- The registrant may <u>terminate</u> a POA at any time by <u>executing a notice of revocation</u>.
- A <u>new POA</u> is only needed if a <u>different person</u> signs the <u>renewal application</u>.
- The POA should be <u>filed</u> at the <u>pharmacy</u> with the executed DEA Form 222 and must be <u>readily retrievable</u> (it is <u>not submitted</u> to the DEA).

Each time a schedule I or II drug changes location, DEA Form 222 or the electronic alternative documents the movement. A copy of Form 222 will accompany the drug during <u>distribution, purchase or transfer</u>. If CSOS is used, the electronic system will trace the drug's movement. A record is needed when a schedule II drug moves from a wholesaler/supplier to a pharmacy, from a pharmacy to another pharmacy or to a reverse distributor for destruction. This documentation is required for every drug movement, except in two situations:

- When the drug is dispensed or administered to a patient.
- When a central fill pharmacy associated with a retail chain is filling schedule II drugs for one of the chain's retail stores.

DEA FORM 222

<u>DEA Form 222</u> is available as both a <u>single-sheet</u> form and a <u>triplicate</u> form with three carbon copies (Copy 1, Copy 2 and Copy 3). The single-sheet Form 222 was released in 2019 to replace the triplicate form. The DEA is allowing a two-year transition period to the single-sheet form. During this time, triplicate forms can still be used to order schedule I and II drugs, but any registrant who requests additional order forms will be issued single-sheet forms. The triplicate forms will not be accepted after October 31, 2021, requiring all registrants to use the single-sheet form or CSOS from that point forward. It is wise to be prepared to answer questions about either on the exam.

The following items are <u>preprinted</u> on Form 222 (an example Form 222 is shown on the following page):

- A <u>serial number</u>, in a consecutive number series
- The <u>pharmacy name and address</u>
- The <u>pharmacy DEA number</u>
- The drug <u>schedules</u> that the pharmacy is <u>permitted to order</u> (i.e., schedules II, III, IV and V)

Each copy of the triplicate form must be retained by the appropriate parties. The table below describes who retains each copy for typical transactions. When using the single-sheet form, each entity involved in the transfer of schedule II drugs must retain a copy of Form 222 (e.g., by making a photocopy of the form).

TRIPLICATE FORM 222 FOR SCHEDULE II DRUG TRANSACTIONS

ACTION	COPY 1 (BROWN)	COPY 2 (GREEN)	COPY 3 (BLUE)
Pharmacy orders drugs from a supplier	Supplier	DEA	Pharmacy
Pharmacy returns unused drugs back to a supplier	Pharmacy	DEA	Supplier
Pharmacy sends unused drugs back to reverse distributor for disposal	Pharmacy	DEA	Reverse distributor
Pharmacy sells or lends drugs to another pharmacy	Supplying pharmacy	DEA	Receiving pharmacy
Pharmacy sells or lends drugs to a physician for administration or dispensing	Pharmacy	DEA	Physician

Single-Sheet DEA Form 222 Example

DEA FORM-222	U.S. OFFICIAL ORDER FORMS - SCHEDULES I & II DRUG ENFORCEMENT ADMINISTRATION	OMB APPROVAL No. 1117-0010

PURCHASER INFORMATION

REGISTRATION INFORMATION

REGISTRATION #:
REGISTERED AS: CHAIN PHARMACY
SCHEDULES: 2,2N,3,3N,4,5
ORDER FORM NUMBER: 200002496
DATE ISSUED: 01012020
ORDER FORM 3 OF 3

SUPPLIER DEA NUMBER:#

PART 2: TO BE FILLED IN BY PURCHASER

BUSINESS NAME

STREET ADDRESS

CITY, STATE, ZIP CODE

PART 1: TO BE FILLED IN BY PURCHASER

Print or Type Name and Title

Signature of Requesting Official (must be authorized to sign order form)   Date

PART 5:
TO BE
FILLED IN BY
PURCHASER

PART 3: ALTERNATE SUPPLIER IDENTIFICATION - to be filled in by first supplier (name in part 2) if order is endorsed to another supplier to fill.

ALTERNATE DEA #

Signature- by first supplier

OFFICIAL AUTHORIZED TO EXECUTE ON BEHALF OF SUPPLIER   DATE

ITEM	NO. OF PACKAGES	PACKAGE SIZE	NAME OF ITEM	NUMBER REC'D	DATE REC'D	PART 4: TO BE FILLED IN BY SUPPLIER NATIONAL DRUG CODE	NUMBER SHIPPED	DATE SHIPPED
1								
2								
3								
4								
5								
6								
7								
8								
9								
10								
11								
12								
13								
14								
15								
16								
17								
18								
19								
20								

← LAST LINE COMPLETED (MUST BE 20 OR LESS)

☞ Source: U.S. Department of Justice

Triplicate DEA Form 222 Example

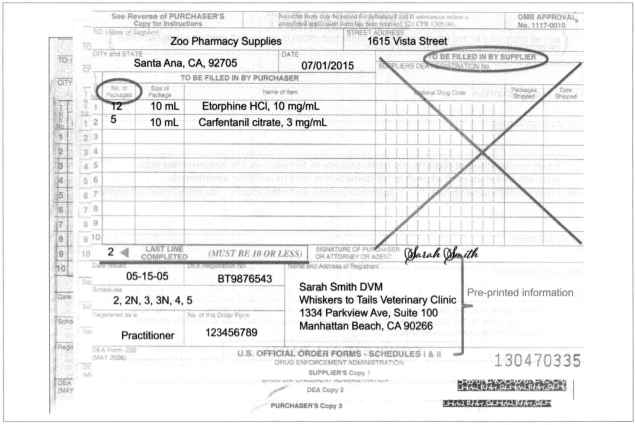

☞ Source: U.S. Department of Justice
☞ ©RxPrep, Inc.

STEPS TO ORDER SCHEDULE II DRUGS WITH FORM 222

PURCHASER

Both Triplicate & Single-Sheet Forms

1. Fill out the name and address of the supplier.

2. Enter the number of packages, size of the package, drug name and strength. Each item must be on a separate line. Do not skip any lines.

3. Write the number of the last line used into the space on the bottom left of the form. This field must be completed.

4. The DEA registrant or person with POA must sign/date the form (handwritten signature and date is required).

5. If a mistake is made, write "VOID" on Form 222 and start over with a new Form 222.

Triplicate Form 222 Differences

- There are 10 lines on each form; a maximum of 10 items can be ordered.
- Keep Copy 3 (blue) and send Copies 1 and 2 (brown and green) to the supplier.
- The first two Copies must stay attached; the supplier cannot fill the order if they are separated.

Single-Sheet Form 222 Differences

- There are 20 lines on each form; a maximum of 20 items can be ordered.
- Make a copy of the form (readily-retrievable electronic copies are allowed) and keep for three years.
- Send the form to the supplier.

SUPPLIER

Both Triplicate & Single-Sheet Forms

1. If any required fields are missing, or if the form is sloppy and not legible, return the form to the purchaser. Minor errors can be corrected.

2. Fill in the NDC, number of containers for each item and the date shipped.

3. If unable to provide the entire quantity, provide a partial shipment and supply the balance within 60 days or endorse (i.e., send) the order to another supplier.

4. Shipments can only be delivered to the DEA-registered address.

5. Deliver the scheduled drugs to the purchaser in a separate container from non-controlled drugs or OTC products.

Triplicate Form 222 Differences

- Keep Copy 1 (brown) and send Copy 2 (green) to the DEA by the end of the month in which the order is filled.

Single-Sheet Form 222 Differences

- Keep the original copy for two years.

PURCHASER

Both Triplicate & Single-Sheet Forms

1. When the order arrives at the pharmacy, it must be checked in by a pharmacist, who records the number of packages and the date received by comparing the delivery to the order.

Triplicate Form 222

- The number of packages and the date received should be recorded on Copy 3 (blue).
- Keep Copy 3 for three years.

Single-Sheet Form 222

- Part 5 (see the form on the previous page) can be completed once the drugs arrive from the supplier. Fill in the number of packages and date received on the pharmacy's photocopy of the form.

ELECTRONIC CONTROLLED SUBSTANCE ORDERING SYSTEM

The Controlled Substance Ordering System (CSOS) is the electronic equivalent to Form 222 and allows for electronic ordering of schedule I and II drugs. CSOS can be used to order schedule III – V drugs, but it is not required. Each person authorized to place orders for schedule I and II drugs must obtain a personal digital certificate to sign orders (e.g., the registrant and any individuals granted POA). Digital certificates cannot be shared.

ADVANTAGES OF CSOS

- Reduced ordering errors
- Decreased paperwork
- Reduced administrative costs
- Faster drug delivery (potential for next day delivery)
- Easy to use, allowing for more frequent ordering

When using CSOS, the purchaser creates an electronic order using DEA-approved software. When the order is complete, the purchaser signs it with their unique digital certificate and electronically transmits it to the supplier. The supplier receives the order, verifies the certificate and fills the order. The supplier must report the transaction to the DEA within two business days from the date the order was filled.

CSOS Order and Supply Chain

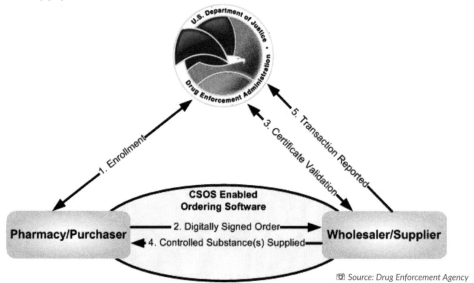

Source: Drug Enforcement Agency

LOST OR STOLEN DEA FORM 222 OR ELECTRONIC ORDERS

If a completed Form 222 is lost or stolen, the purchaser must resubmit the order with a new Form 222 and submit it to the supplier. The pharmacy must provide a statement to the distributor with the new Form 222 containing the following information:

- The serial number of the original form
- The date of the initial order
- A statement that the controlled substances were not received

  - The pharmacy must keep a copy of this statement with a copy of the initial order and the second order.

If unused forms are discovered to be lost or stolen, the pharmacy must immediately notify the local DEA Diversion Field Office. The serial number for each lost or stolen form must be provided unless an entire book or multiple books of forms are missing, and the serial numbers are unknown. If the serial numbers are unknown, then the pharmacy must provide the approximate date that the DEA issued the forms.

If an electronic order is lost, the purchaser must provide a signed statement to the supplier stating that the fulfilled order was not received. This statement must contain the unique tracking number and the date of the lost order. If a replacement order is created, the purchaser must electronically link the new order with the record of the lost order and the signed statement.

DISTRIBUTION OF CONTROLLED SUBSTANCES BETWEEN DEA REGISTRANTS

A pharmacy can transfer controlled substances to another pharmacy, the original supplier or the manufacturer. A DEA Form 222 or CSOS must be used to transfer schedule I and II drugs. An invoice or CSOS is used to transfer schedule III – V drugs and must contain the following information:

- Drug name, dosage form, strength and quantity
- Date of controlled substance transfer
- Recipient's name, address and DEA number

All records of these transfers (inventory, Form 222, invoice) must be kept for at least three years.

Pharmacy Going Out of Business

If a pharmacy goes out of business or is acquired by new ownership, the pharmacy can transfer controlled substances to the new pharmacy, once the DEA number is confirmed. A complete inventory is taken and used as the transferring registrant's final inventory and as the initial inventory for the acquiring registrant. The inventory is not sent to the DEA. Each pharmacy must maintain a copy of the inventory records for at least three years. Inventories are taken at either the opening or closing of the business day, and the time taken (opening or closing) must be recorded on the inventory.

Pharmacy Selling Controlled Substances

A pharmacy can sell controlled substances to other pharmacies or prescribers without registering as a distributor, provided both parties are registered with the DEA to dispense controlled substances. The total quantity sold cannot exceed 5% of the total quantity dispensed each year by the selling pharmacy. If a pharmacy is selling schedule II drugs, a Form 222 must be used. The pharmacy selling the schedule II drugs is responsible for forwarding Copy 2 of the Form 222 to the DEA by the end of the month.

A healthcare practitioner cannot write a prescription to obtain controlled substances for the purpose of stocking them for "office use" or to dispense directly to patients. The practitioner would need to purchase the controlled substances from a pharmacy or wholesaler.

CANCELLING OR VOIDING CONTROLLED SUBSTANCE ORDERS

A purchaser can cancel all or part of a controlled substance order by notifying the supplier in writing. The supplier must indicate the cancellation on Form 222 (Copies 1 and 2 of the triplicate form) by drawing a line through the canceled item/s and writing "canceled" in the space for the number of items shipped.

A supplier can void part or all of an order by notifying the purchaser in writing. The supplier must draw a line through the canceled items on Form 222 (Copies 1 and 2 of the triplicate form) and print "void" in the space for the number of items shipped. Alternatively, if the supplier cannot fulfill an order, they can endorse (i.e., transfer) the order to another supplier that can fulfill it. This only applies if the order was placed using a paper Form 222. If Form 222 is illegible, incomplete or altered, the supplier returns Copies 1 and 2 to the purchaser with the rationale for not filling the order. The purchaser must keep the original Form 222 (all three copies of the triplicate form).

An electronic order is invalid if any required data field is empty, if it is not signed with a DEA-sanctioned digital certificate, if the digital certificate is expired or if the purchaser's digital signature is not validated. The supplier can refuse to fill an order for any reason and must provide the purchaser with a statement of the occurrence. The purchaser must electronically link this statement to the original order. Invalid electronic orders cannot be corrected; the purchaser must submit a new order.

The supplier is not required to keep a record of unfilled orders, but the purchaser must keep an electronic copy of the voided order. If a supplier partially voids an order, the supplier must indicate nothing was shipped for each voided item in the linked record.

CONTROLLED SUBSTANCE LOSS OR THEFT

A pharmacy must report a significant loss or theft of controlled substances to the local DEA office, in writing, within one business day of discovery.[197] After initially notifying the DEA, the pharmacy must conduct an investigation and submit Form 106 to the DEA with the findings. If the investigation determines that theft or loss did not occur, then Form 106 does not need to be submitted. Instead, the registrant must notify the DEA in writing that there was no theft or loss.[198]

CONSIDERATIONS TO DETERMINE IF LOSS OR THEFT IS SIGNIFICANT

- The specific substances lost or stolen and their likelihood for diversion
- The quantity lost in relation to the type of business
- The individuals with access to the lost or stolen drug
- History or pattern of losses or local diversion issues
- Unique circumstances surrounding the loss or theft

Pharmacists must also report all controlled substance drug losses to the California Board of Pharmacy within 14 calendar days for losses due to licensed employee theft[199] or 30 calendar days for any other type of loss.[200] A copy of the DEA Form 106 can be sent to the board of pharmacy.[201]

197   21 CFR § 1301.74(c)
198   https://www.deadiversion.usdoj.gov/fed_regs/rules/2003/fr0708.htm (accessed 2020 Nov 13)
199   B&PC 4104
200   CCR 1715.6
201   http://www.pharmacy.ca.gov/licensees/facility/dea106.shtml (accessed 2020 Nov 13)

DEA Form 106 Example

DEA FORM 106 **Report of Theft or Loss of Controlled Substances**

OMB No. 1117-0001 (Exp. Date 7/31/2023)

U.S. Department of Justice
Drug Enforcement Administration
Diversion Control Division

Type of Report: *(check one box only)* ☐ New Report ☐ Amendment Key *(prior report dated)*: _____

1. **DEA Registration Number:** _____

   Name of Business: _____

   Address: _____

   City: _____ **State:** _____ **ZIP Code:** _____

   Point of Contact: _____

   Email Address: _____ **Phone No.:** _____

Date of the Theft or Loss *(or first discovery of theft or loss)*: _____ **Number of Thefts and Losses in the past 24 months:** _____

Principal Business of Registrant: ☐Pharmacy ☐Practitioner ☐Manufacturer ☐Hospital/Clinic ☐Distributor ☐NTP ☐Other (Specify) _____

---

2. **Type of Theft or Loss:** -

---

3. **Loss in Transit.** *(*Fill out this section only if there was a loss in transit, or hijacking of transport vehicle.)*

   Name of Common Carrier: _____

   Telephone Number of Common Carrier: _____ Package Tracking Number: _____

   Have there been losses in transit from this same carrier in the past? ☐ No ☐ Yes *(If yes, how many, excluding this theft or loss?)*: _____

   Was the package received and accepted by the consignee? ☐ No ☐ Yes *(If yes, the consignee is responsible for reporting the theft or loss.)*

   If the package was accepted by the consignee, did it appear to be tampered with? ☐ No ☐ Yes

   Name of Consignee / Supplier: _____
   Enter the Name of Consignee (if reported by the supplier), or the Name of Supplier (if the package was accepted by the consignee).
   If the consignee does not have a DEA Registration Number, e.g. if this was a shipment to a patient, or a nursing home emergency kit, enter "Patient" or "Nursing Home Kit."

   DEA Registration Number of Consignee / Supplier: _____
   Enter the DEA Registration Number of Consignee (if reported by the supplier), or DEA Registration Number of Supplier, (if the package was accepted by the consignee). If the controlled substances were shipped to a non-registrant, leave blank, unless a registered pharmacy shipped to an emergency kit held on site at a nursing home. In this case, the supplying pharmacy is required to report the theft or loss.

---

4. If this was a robbery, were any people injured? ☐ No ☐ Yes *(If yes, how many?)*: _____ Were any people killed? ☐ No ☐ Yes *(If yes, how many?)*: _____

---

5. **What is the total value of the controlled substances stolen or lost?:** $ _____
   (This is the amount you paid for the controlled substances, not the retail value.)

---

6. **Was theft reported to Police?** ☐ No ☐ Yes *(If yes, fill out the following information)*:

   Name of Police Department: _____ Police Report number: _____

   Name of Responding Officer: _____ Phone No.: _____

---

7. **Which corrective measure(s) have you taken to prevent a future theft or loss?**

   ☐ Installed monitoring equipment (e.g. video camera).   ☐ Provided security training to staff.

   ☐ Increased employee monitoring (e.g. random drug tests).   ☐ Requested increased security patrols by Police.

   ☐ Installed metal bars or other security on doors or windows.   ☐ Hired security guards for premises.

   ☐ Secured Controlled Substances within safe.   ☐ Terminated employee.

   ☐ Other (Please describe on last page).

---

8. **Were any pharmaceuticals or merchandise taken?**   ☐ No   ☐ Yes *(Estimated Value)*:

Form DEA-106 Pg. 1

Source: U.S. Department of Justice

Reporting In-Transit Losses

The loss or theft of controlled substances in-transit (i.e., deliveries) must be reported to the DEA verbally immediately and in writing within three days. The supplier is responsible for reporting this loss to the DEA. The pharmacy is only responsible for making the report if the registrant has already signed for the delivery and subsequently notices that some or all of the controlled substances are missing. The report must include the date of the shipment and the name of the carrier or the delivery personnel.

DISPOSAL OF CONTROLLED SUBSTANCES

A registrant (e.g., pharmacy or dispensing prescriber) should not send drugs to the DEA for disposal unless they have received prior approval from the local DEA field office. Otherwise, controlled substances should be disposed of using one of the methods discussed below.

REGISTRANTS RETURNING CONTROLLED SUBSTANCES TO THE SUPPLIER

Pharmacies can return controlled substances to the drug supplier or manufacturer. The pharmacist must maintain a written record of the return showing:

- The date of the transaction
- The name, strength, dosage form and quantity of the controlled substance
- The supplier or manufacturer's name, address and registration number

A new Form 222 or its electronic equivalent must accompany the return of schedule II drugs. The supplier or manufacturer receiving the controlled substances must initiate the order. If the triplicate form is used, the supplier or manufacturer will keep Copy 3 and send Copies 1 and 2 to the pharmacy, which is acting as the "supplier." The pharmacy will forward Copy 2 to the DEA.

REGISTRANTS SENDING CONTROLLED SUBSTANCES TO A REVERSE DISTRIBUTOR

A reverse distributor is a company that disposes of controlled substances. A pharmacy can send controlled substances to a reverse distributor for disposal, provided the reverse distributor is registered with the DEA.

The reverse distributor must issue Form 222 or the electronic equivalent to a pharmacy that is transferring schedule II drugs for disposal. If the triplicate form is used, the reverse distributor will keep Copy 3 and send Copies 1 and 2 to the pharmacy, which is acting as the "supplier." The pharmacy will forward Copy 2 to the DEA. If the pharmacy is transferring schedule III – V drugs, then a record (e.g., a receipt or invoice) must be maintained with the following information: drug name, dosage form, strength, quantity and date transferred.

DEA Form 41 is used to document the destruction of controlled substances. The reverse distributor will submit Form 41 to the DEA once the controlled substances have been destroyed.[202]

---

202   http://www.deadiversion.usdoj.gov/21cfr_reports/surrend/41_form.pdf (accessed 2020 Nov 13)

DEA Form 41 Example

OMB APPROVAL NO. 1117-0007 Expiration Date 10/31/2020

U. S. DEPARTMENT OF JUSTICE – DRUG ENFORCEMENT ADMINISTRATION
REGISTRANT RECORD OF CONTROLLED SUBSTANCES DESTROYED
FORM DEA-41

A. REGISTRANT INFORMATION

Registered Name:	DEA Registration Number:
Registered Address:	
City: State:	Zip Code:
Telephone Number:	Contact Name:

B. ITEM DESTROYED
1. Inventory

	National Drug Code or DEA Controlled Substances Code Number	Batch Number	Name of Substance	Strength	Form	Pkg. Qty.	Number of Full Pkgs.	Partial Pkg. Count	Total Destroyed
Examples	16590-598-60	N/A	Kadian	60mg	Capsules	60	2	0	120 Capsules
	0555-0767-02	N/A	Adderall	5mg	Tablet	100	0	83	83 Tablets
	9050	B02120312	Codeine	N/A	Bulk	1.25 kg	N/A	N/A	1.25 kg
1.									
2.									
3.									
4.									
5.									
6.									
7.									

2. Collected Substances

	Returned Mail-Back Package	Sealed Inner Liner	Unique Identification Number	Size of Sealed Inner Liner	Quantity of Packages(s)/Liner(s) Destroyed
Examples	X		MBP1106, MBP1108 - MBP1110, MBP112	N/A	5
		X	CRL1007 - CRL1027	15 gallon	21
		X	CRL1201	5 gallon	1
1.					
2.					
3.					
4.					
5.					
6.					
7.					

Form DEA-41   *See instructions on reverse (page 2) of form.*

Source: U.S. Department of Justice

CONTROLLED SUBSTANCES PART 3:
PRESCRIBING AND DISPENSING

CHAPTER CONTENTS

Healthcare Providers Authorized to Prescribe Controlled Substances **116**
Controlled Substance Prescription Requirements **117**
Valid DEA Numbers 117
Corresponding Responsibility and Red Flags to Prevent Diversion 118
Controlled Substance Utilization Review and Evaluation System 119
Valid Controlled Substance Prescriptions **120**
Out-of-State Prescriptions 120
Written Prescriptions and California Security Forms 120
Oral Prescriptions 123
Faxed Prescriptions 123
Electronic Prescriptions 124
Errors or Omissions 124
Medicare Part D Opioid Limits on Initial Prescriptions 125
Schedule II Prescriptions **125**
Multiple Prescriptions for Schedule II Drugs 125
Partial Filling of Schedule II Prescriptions 125
Emergency Filling of Schedule II Drugs 127
Schedule III – V Prescriptions **127**
Recordkeeping Requirements for Schedule III – V Refills..128
Partial Fills of Schedule III – V Prescriptions..128
Emergency Filling of Schedule III – V Drugs 128
Transferring Controlled Substances Prescriptions.. **128**
Warning Labels for Controlled Substances.. **129**
California Label Requirements 129
Dispensing and Delivering Controlled Substances to Patients **129**
Treatment of Opioid Dependence **130**
Opioid Treatment Programs...130
Opioid Dependence Treatment in an Office-Based Setting 131
Products with Restricted Sales **132**
Pseudoephedrine, Ephedrine, Phenylpropanolamine and Norpseudoephedrine 132
Dextromethorphan 133
Hypodermic Needles and Syringes 134

CHAPTER 7
CONTROLLED SUBSTANCES PART 3:
PRESCRIBING AND DISPENSING

HEALTHCARE PROVIDERS AUTHORIZED TO PRESCRIBE CONTROLLED SUBSTANCES

A prescription for a controlled substance for a legitimate medical purpose may only be issued by a physician (MD/DO), dentist (DDS/DMD), podiatrist (DPM), veterinarian (DVM), mid-level practitioner (MLP) or other registered practitioner who is:

- Authorized to prescribe controlled substances by the jurisdiction or state in which the practitioner is licensed to practice.
- Registered or exempt from DEA registration.
- An agent or employee of a hospital or institution acting in the normal course of business under the DEA registration of the hospital or institution.

Physicians, dentists, veterinarians, podiatrists and optometrists are healthcare providers who can <u>prescribe</u> controlled substances <u>independently</u> within their <u>scope of practice</u>. MLPs must prescribe under a physician-directed protocol. The specific medications they are authorized to prescribe will vary depending on the agreement with the physician. See the Pharmacy Practice Part 1 chapter for additional information regarding prescriptive authority.

MID-LEVEL PRACTITIONER PRESCRIBING AUTHORITY

PRACTITIONER TYPE	CONTROLLED SUBSTANCE PRESCRIBING AUTHORITY
Nurse Practitioners (NP)	Schedule II – V
Physician Assistants (PA)	Schedule II – V
Registered Pharmacists (RPh)	Schedule II – V
Naturopathic Doctors (ND)	Schedule III – V (does not include schedule II)

CONTROLLED SUBSTANCE PRESCRIPTION REQUIREMENTS

VALID DEA NUMBERS

Each DEA number is unique and is assigned to an individual healthcare provider or an institution. The DEA number permits the individual to write controlled substance prescriptions and authorizes an institution to order and manage controlled substances. Each DEA number is randomly generated and consists of the following:

- Starts with <u>two letters</u>
  - ❑ <u>First letter</u>: identifies the <u>type</u> of practitioner or institution (i.e., registrant type)
  - ❑ <u>Second letter</u>: first letter of the <u>prescriber's last name</u>
- Letters are followed by <u>seven numbers</u>

Last number is the "<u>check digit</u>" (see the Study Tip on the following page)

If a practitioner is authorized to <u>prescribe narcotics</u> (such as buprenorphine) for <u>opioid addiction treatment</u>, the practitioner will receive a <u>DATA 2000 waiver</u> unique identification number (UIN). The number is the same as the practitioner's DEA number, except that the letter "<u>X</u>" replaces the <u>first letter</u>.

- For example: Wendy Clark, MD is assigned the DEA number AC2143799.
  - ❑ A is the initial letter, which represents the registrant type (physician).
  - ❑ C is for her last name (Clark).
  - ❑ If Dr. Clark becomes a DATA 2000 waivered practitioner, her UIN would be XC2143799.

Prescribers in a hospital or other institution, including medical <u>interns, residents</u> and visiting physicians, can prescribe medication under the <u>DEA registration</u> of that <u>hospital or institution</u>. The hospital or institution will assign a specific internal code number to each practitioner authorized to prescribe. The internal code number will follow the last number of the hospital's DEA number. For example:

- A hospital's DEA number is AB1234567 and a resident is assigned the internal code number "012."
- The resident would use "AB1234567-012" as their DEA number when prescribing controlled substances.

FIRST LETTER OF DEA NUMBER FOR EACH REGISTRANT TYPE
A/B/F/G: Hospital, clinic, practitioner, teaching institution, pharmacy
M: Mid-level practitioner (e.g., nurse practitioner, physician assistant, optometrist)
P/R: Manufacturer, distributor, researcher, analytical lab, importer, exporter, reverse distributor, narcotic treatment program
X: DATA-waived practitioner

DETERMINING THE VALIDITY OF A DEA NUMBER

Step one: Add the 1st, 3rd and 5th digits together.

Step two: Add the 2nd, 4th and 6th digits together.

Step three: Multiply the result of step two by 2.

Step four: Add the results of step one and step three together. The last digit of this sum should match the last digit of the prescriber's DEA number. This is called the "check digit."

Example: Verify the following DEA number: BT6835752

Step one: 6 + 3 + 7 = 16
Step two: 8 + 5 + 5 = 18
Step three: 18 x 2 = 36
Step four: 16 + 36 = 5<u>2</u>

The last digit of the sum in step four is 2. This should be the same as the last digit of the DEA number. Therefore, this DEA number appears to be valid.

Practice: Verify Dr. Mikacich's DEA number (BM6125341):

Step one: _____

Step two: _____

Step three: _____

Step four: _____

The last digit of the sum in step four is: _____

Does Dr. Mikacich's DEA number appear to be valid?* Yes / No

*Answer: Yes

CORRESPONDING RESPONSIBILITY AND RED FLAGS TO PREVENT DIVERSION

In order for a prescription to be considered <u>valid</u>, it must be issued in the <u>usual course of professional treatment</u> for a <u>legitimate medical purpose</u>. The condition being treated must be one that the prescriber would be expected to treat. The <u>pharmacist</u> has a <u>corresponding responsibility</u> to ensure a controlled substance <u>prescription</u> is <u>valid</u> prior to filling. A pharmacist is <u>not required to dispense</u> a prescription if he/she has any concerns about the legitimacy. If a pharmacist dispenses a controlled substance prescription that he/she suspects has not been issued for a legitimate medical purpose, then the pharmacist and prescriber may both be prosecuted.

Pharmacists should be aware of potential "red flags" when filling controlled substance prescriptions to help prevent drug abuse and diversion. See examples from the NABP in the Study Tip on the following page. Additional signs of drug abuse or misuse may include: irregularities on the face of the prescription, prescriptions for unusually large quantities or an initial prescription for a strong opioid.

NABP "RED FLAGS" OF DIVERSION

- Frequent requests for early refills
- Prescriber and/or patient located an unusual distance from pharmacy
- Patient profile reveals multiple prescribers for duplicate therapy (e.g., "doctor shopping")
- Similar or identical prescriptions for multiple patients from same prescriber (e.g., "pill mill")
- Prescription is not within prescriber's scope of practice (e.g., opioid analgesic from a psychiatrist)

- Patients presenting to the pharmacy in groups
- Unusual patient behavior (e.g., nervous demeanor)
- Patient pays cash for an opioid prescription
- Use of street slang to refer to a medication (e.g., "zannies" for *Xanax*)
- Patient is prescribed a "drug cocktail" (e.g., opioid + benzodiazepine + muscle relaxant)
- A pending federal or state action against prescriber

Secure Storage for Patients for Scheduled Drugs

Many drugs that are used illicitly, including opioids, are stolen from another family member. Community pharmacies that dispense schedule II, III and IV drugs must have medication lock boxes or medication locks available for purchase. The products should have a locking mechanism, such as a password or key and they should be displayed near the pharmacy. Pharmacies where a licensed pharmacist is the majority owner and manager of no more than four pharmacies are exempt from this law.

CONTROLLED SUBSTANCE UTILIZATION REVIEW AND EVALUATION SYSTEM

The Controlled Substance Utilization Review and Evaluation System (CURES) is California's Prescription Drug Monitoring Program (PDMP). Prescribers and pharmacists can access CURES to review all schedule II – V drugs that have been prescribed and dispensed for a given patient. A prescriber can request from CURES a list of all patients that have designated them as their prescriber. A patient report lists all scheduled drugs the patient has received, the prescribers, the dispensing pharmacies and other dispensing information. Each pharmacy must submit dispensing data for schedule II – V drugs to CURES within one working day after the prescription was dispensed.[203] All California pharmacists with active licenses must be registered to access CURES.[204]

Prescribers must check CURES to review a patient's history for the past twelve months before prescribing schedule II – IV drugs for the first time and at least every six months thereafter. Pharmacists are not mandated, but highly encouraged, to check CURES before dispensing schedule II – IV prescriptions.

A practitioner must review a patient's history in the CURES database no earlier than 24 hours, or on the previous business day, before prescribing, ordering or administering a schedule II – IV drug for the first time, and every six months if the drug is still being used.[205] There are some exceptions (e.g., a CURES review is not required for veterinarians).

203   H&SC 11165(d)
204   H&SC 11165.1(a)(1)(A)(ii)
205   H&SC 11165.4(a)(2)

VALID CONTROLLED SUBSTANCE PRESCRIPTIONS

All controlled substance <u>prescriptions</u> are <u>valid for six months</u> and must include the prescriber's <u>DEA number</u>. A controlled substance prescription must be <u>dated</u> and <u>signed</u> by the prescriber on the <u>date</u> it is <u>issued</u> to the patient.[206] Pre-signing prescription blanks is illegal and has resulted in disciplinary action and suspension of the prescriber's medical license. Pharmacists should not fill prescriptions that are suspected to be pre-signed.

Any agent of the prescriber (e.g., nurse or office staff) can orally or electronically transmit a prescription for a schedule III – V drug. The name of the agent transmitting the prescription must be recorded.[207]

OUT-OF-STATE PRESCRIPTIONS

In order to fill a controlled substance from an <u>out-of-state prescriber</u>, the prescription must meet the controlled substance prescription requirements of the state in which the prescriber practices and the prescriber must be registered with the DEA. The schedule of the drug will determine if the prescription can be dispensed directly to the patient at the pharmacy or mailed to the patient.

- <u>Schedule II drugs</u>: a California pharmacy can fill the prescription but it can <u>only be delivered</u> (mailed) to an out-of-state patient (i.e., the drug cannot be dispensed directly to the patient at the pharmacy).

- <u>Schedule III – V drugs</u>: a California pharmacy may <u>dispense</u> the prescription <u>directly</u> to the patient or <u>deliver it by mail</u>.[208]

WRITTEN PRESCRIPTIONS AND CALIFORNIA SECURITY FORMS

A <u>California security form</u> must be used for <u>all written controlled substance prescriptions</u> (schedules II – V), with a couple of exceptions, as discussed later in this chapter.[209] Prescribers can write a prescription for both <u>controlled</u> and <u>non-controlled</u> drugs on the security forms or they can choose to use separate forms for each type.

A California security prescription form must have the following features:

- The word "<u>void</u>" appears across the front of the prescription when photocopied or scanned due to the heat exposure.

- A <u>chemical void protection</u> that prevents alteration via chemical washing.

- A <u>watermark</u> is printed on the back of the prescription blank that reads "California Security Prescription." Watermarks are not duplicated by copy machines.

- A feature printed in <u>thermochromic ink</u> which reacts to changes in temperature. Commonly, if a thermochromic image is touched or blown on it will disappear and reappear after it cools. This effect is not duplicated by copy machines.

- An area of <u>opaque writing</u> that causes the writing to disappear if the prescription is lightened.

---

206   *H&SC 11164(a)(1)*
207   *H&SC 11164(b)(3)*
208   *H&SC 11164.1(b)*
209   *H&SC 11167*

- A <u>description</u> of the security features included on each form.
- Six <u>quantity check-off boxes</u> printed on the form.
  - ❏ Must have the following quantities: 1-24, 25-49, 50-74, 75-100, 101-150, 151 and over.
  - ❏ Must be <u>checked by the prescriber</u> to <u>correspond</u> to the written <u>quantity</u> of the drug.
- A space to designate the <u>units</u> referenced in the quantity boxes when the drug is not in tablet or capsule form (e.g., mL).
- Statement that the "Prescription is void if the number of drugs prescribed is not noted."
- The <u>preprinted</u> name, licensure category, license number and DEA number of the prescriber.
- <u>Check boxes</u> that indicate the <u>number of refills</u> ordered.
- The date of issue.
- A <u>check box</u> indicating the prescriber's order <u>not to substitute</u>.
- A <u>check box</u> by each prescriber's name when a prescription form lists <u>multiple prescribers</u>. A prescriber who signs a multiple prescriber form will need to check the box by his or her name.
- An identifying number assigned to the approved security printer by the Department of Justice.
- A <u>unique serial number</u> on <u>each</u> security form, which permits the form to be traced. The number has 15 digits (3 letters followed by 12 numbers). The prescriber's serial numbers are reported to CURES.

Each batch of security prescription forms has a <u>lot number</u> printed on the form. The forms are printed sequentially, beginning with the number one.

There are an increasing number of inappropriate security forms being brought into pharmacies, and an increasing number of stolen security forms. The board posts on its website confirmed notices of stolen or compromised security prescription forms that have been reported by prescribers. A list of these can be viewed on the board's website.[210]

Multiple Prescriber Forms for Hospitals and Other Institutions

Hospitals often have physicians from the surrounding community who are granted privileges to see their patients at the hospital. Many hospitals have medical residents rotating through the facility for short periods of time. Both types of prescribers need to write prescriptions, but may not have their own forms for each hospital in which they work. For this purpose, the boards of medicine and pharmacy permit a <u>designated prescriber</u> at a facility that has <u>25 or more physicians</u> to order security prescription forms for their facility that <u>do not include</u> the <u>preprinted prescriber information</u> (prescriber's name, category of licensure, license number, DEA number and address of the prescribing practitioner).[211] These security forms will be signed out by the designated prescriber in a record book that includes the name to whom they were given, the category of license and number, the DEA number and the quantity of security forms issued. The record must be kept in the health facility for <u>three years</u>.

210   http://www.pharmacy.ca.gov/licensees/stolen_fraudulent_rx_forms.shtml (accessed 2020 Nov 13)
211   H&SC 11162.1(c)

Single Prescriber, Single Drug Form

Single Prescriber, Multiple Drug Form

Multiple Prescriber Form

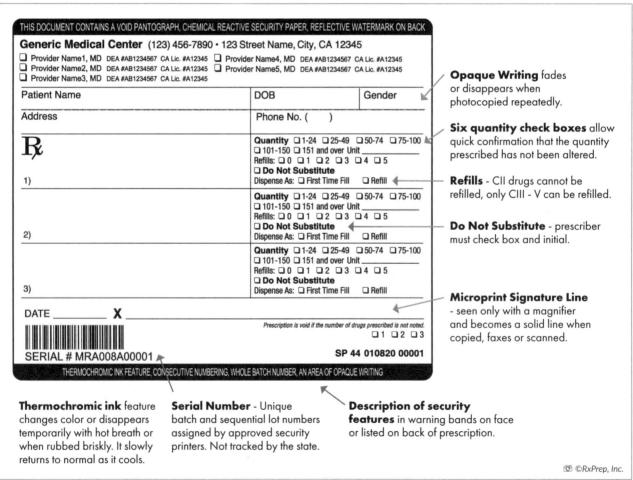

Opaque Writing fades or disappears when photocopied repeatedly.

Six quantity check boxes allow quick confirmation that the quantity prescribed has not been altered.

Refills - CII drugs cannot be refilled, only CIII - V can be refilled.

Do Not Substitute - prescriber must check box and initial.

Microprint Signature Line - seen only with a magnifier and becomes a solid line when copied, faxes or scanned.

Thermochromic ink feature changes color or disappears temporarily with hot breath or when rubbed briskly. It slowly returns to normal as it cools.

Serial Number - Unique batch and sequential lot numbers assigned by approved security printers. Not tracked by the state.

Description of security features in warning bands on face or listed on back of prescription.

©RxPrep, Inc.

Forms courtesy of Minuteman Press.

Exceptions to Using the California Security Form

A prescription for a controlled substance is exempt from using a security form in two instances:

- A patient is terminally ill (i.e., life expectancy ≤ 1 year) and the prescription is for medication to manage pain/other symptoms of the terminal illness.
  - ❑ The prescriber must write "11159.2 exemption" on the prescription form used.
- During a declared emergency when the California Board of Pharmacy has issued a notice of this exemption.
  - ❑ The prescriber must write "11159.3 exemption" or a similar statement indicating the patient is affected by the declared emergency.
  - ❑ No more than a seven-day supply can be dispensed for a schedule II drug.
  - ❑ Prescriptions filled pursuant to this exemption cannot be refilled.

ORAL PRESCRIPTIONS

A pharmacy can accept schedule III – V prescriptions verbally (over the phone) if the pharmacist reduces the prescription to writing (i.e., writes the prescription on the pharmacy's prescription form). The prescription must include all information required for a valid prescription (with the exception of the prescriber's signature). Oral prescriptions for schedule II drugs are not valid except in emergency situations, which is discussed later in this chapter.

FAXED PRESCRIPTIONS

Faxed prescriptions are acceptable for schedule III – V drugs as long as all information required for a valid prescription is included and the prescriber manually signs the fax before sending it to the pharmacy. Prescribers should use a regular prescription form to write for schedule III – V drugs before faxing it to the pharmacy. If the prescriber uses a security form, the text "VOID" (written in thermochromic ink) can appear due to the heat emitted by the fax machine during transmission. This is acceptable to fill as long as the pharmacist validates the faxed prescription by contacting the prescriber's office for verification.

In general, faxed prescriptions for schedule II drugs cannot serve as the original prescription. However, a prescriber can provide a patient with a written prescription for a schedule II drug and fax the same prescription to the pharmacy in order to alert the pharmacy that the patient is on the way. This allows the pharmacy to fill the prescription before the patient arrives. The pharmacist cannot dispense the schedule II drug to the patient until the patient brings the written prescription to the pharmacy and it is verified against the faxed prescription before dispensing.[212] It is not acceptable, even as an alert, for patients to fax prescriptions to a pharmacy.

The only time a faxed prescription for a schedule II drug is valid is if it is written for a patient of a licensed skilled nursing facility, an intermediate care facility, a home health agency or a hospice facility. The pharmacist will need to produce, sign and date a hard copy of the prescription before filling it.[213]

212　21 CFR 1306.11(a)
213　H&SC 11167.5

ELECTRONIC PRESCRIPTIONS

When prescriptions are electronically transmitted entirely through software, safeguards must be in place to prevent unauthorized persons from hacking into the system and illegally transmitting controlled substance prescriptions. In 2010, the DEA released final rules that permit electronic prescriptions for controlled substances (EPCS) for schedule II – V drugs.

Prescribers and pharmacies must use DEA-approved software to send and receive EPCS. The credentials that are permitted for DEA-sanctioned validation will be two of the following factors:[214]

- Something you know (e.g., password or response to a question).
- Something you have (e.g., hard token containing a cryptographic key stored on a hardware device separate from the computer being accessed).
- Something you are (biometric information, such as an iris or fingerprint scan).

Knowledge factors are easily observed, guessed, hacked and used without the practitioner's knowledge. This is why a hard token or biometric information must be used as well. Prescribers must use a two-factor authentication method to sign and transmit EPCS. As an alternative to using two-factor authentication to sign the EPCS, the prescriber can use a digital certificate. A digital certificate contains the user's credentials and is issued by the DEA.

In California, all prescriptions for controlled and non-controlled drugs must be transmitted electronically (i.e., e-prescriptions) by Jan. 1, 2022, unless specified exceptions are met.

ERRORS OR OMISSIONS

All prescriptions for controlled substances must be signed and dated by the prescriber.[215] However, if the date is printed out on a prescription, the prescriber only needs to sign the form. Controlled substance prescriptions that have not been signed and dated cannot be filled.

For schedule II drugs, the pharmacist cannot make any changes to:

- Issue date
- Prescriber name
- Prescriber signature
- Patient name
- Drug name

Minor misspellings can be revised at the pharmacist's discretion. The pharmacist or intern can make changes to any other information on the prescription as long as the pharmacist verifies the change with the prescriber first. It is acceptable to verify with the prescriber if the "void if quantity is not indicated" has not been completed. The pharmacist can complete the form and fill the prescription when reasonable.

214   http://www.deadiversion.usdoj.gov/ecomm/e_rx/faq/practitioners.htm (accessed 2020 Nov 13)
215   H&SC 11164(a)(1)

MEDICARE PART D OPIOID LIMITS ON INITIAL PRESCRIPTIONS

In an attempt to keep patients off long-term opioids, <u>Medicare Part D</u> has limited initial opioid prescriptions to a <u>seven-day supply</u>. The prescription is considered "initial" if the patient has not received any opioid in the last 60 – 90 days.

SCHEDULE II PRESCRIPTIONS

MULTIPLE PRESCRIPTIONS FOR SCHEDULE II DRUGS

Prescriptions for <u>schedule II</u> drugs <u>cannot be refilled</u> even though some patients may require schedule II drugs as maintenance therapy. While there are no federal quantity limits, providers generally avoid prescribing more than a 30-day supply for schedule II drugs due to the risk of abuse and misuse. The inability to provide refills for patients requiring chronic treatment (such as stimulants for ADHD) necessitates frequent office visits. This can become costly and inconvenient for the patient.

In 2007, the DEA authorized prescribers to issue <u>multiple prescriptions</u> at <u>one time</u> for <u>schedule II drugs</u>. These prescriptions can be <u>filled sequentially</u> but <u>cannot exceed a 90-day supply</u>. The prescription <u>cannot be post-dated</u>. Instead, the prescriber must include two dates on each prescription: the <u>date</u> the prescription is <u>written</u> (i.e., the issue date), and the <u>earliest acceptable fill date</u>. The prescriber can write any phrase to indicate the earliest fill date, such as "Do not fill before" or "Do not fill until." This is necessary to prevent a patient from filling the prescriptions at the same time at multiple pharmacies.

For example, if a patient was seen on April 1, 2020, the prescriber can provide the patient with three identical prescriptions, each for a 30-day supply of the schedule II drug, and all dated with the issue date of April 1, 2020. The first prescription can be filled on the day it was written (April 1, 2020), the second prescription will include the earliest possible fill date ("Do not fill until May 1, 2020") and the third prescription will include the earliest possible fill date ("Do not fill until May 31, 2020").

PARTIAL FILLING OF SCHEDULE II PRESCRIPTIONS

The DEA allows for scenarios in which a schedule II prescription may be partially filled.[216,217,218] Similar to partial filling of any other drug, the total <u>quantity dispensed</u> from all partial fills <u>cannot exceed</u> the <u>total quantity prescribed</u>. When a pharmacist fills less than the full amount prescribed, he or she must document the quantity dispensed on the prescription. The remaining balance must be filled within a specific time frame; otherwise, the remaining balance is forfeited.

---

216   21 CFR § 1306.13(a)
217   21 USC § 829(f)
218   Warren, Elizabeth, et al. "DEA Partial Fill Letter." Received by Robert Patterson, 21 Dec. 2017.

There are three circumstances in which a <u>schedule II</u> prescription <u>may be partially filled</u>:

1. If the <u>pharmacy cannot supply</u> the full quantity, a portion of the prescription can be dispensed to hold the patient over until the remaining balance can be obtained.

   ❑ This partial fill can be provided pursuant to a <u>written</u> or an <u>emergency oral prescription</u>.

   ❑ The <u>quantity supplied</u> must be <u>documented</u> on the face of the hard copy or in the electronic prescription record.

   ❑ The remaining portion must be filled within <u>72 hours</u> of the first partial filling. After 72 hours, a <u>new prescription</u> is <u>required</u>.

   ❑ If the <u>remaining</u> portion is <u>not</u> or cannot be <u>filled</u> within <u>72 hours</u> of the first partial filling, the pharmacist must <u>notify the prescriber</u>.

2. Under the 2016 Comprehensive Addiction and Recovery Act (CARA), pharmacists can partially fill schedule II drugs at the <u>request</u> of the <u>patient or prescriber</u>. This was enacted to help prevent stockpiling of unused schedule II drugs, which can lead to misuse or abuse.

   ❑ <u>Additional partial fills</u> can only be dispensed up to <u>30 days</u> from the <u>date</u> the <u>prescription</u> was <u>issued</u>.

   ❑ There is <u>no limit</u> on the <u>number of partial fills</u> a patient can receive pursuant to one prescription, as long as the total quantity dispensed does not exceed the total quantity prescribed.

3. Schedule II prescriptions can be partially filled for patients residing in a <u>LTCF</u> or patients diagnosed with a <u>terminal illness</u> (e.g., hospice patients). This is to reduce drug diversion and waste that can occur if the patient expires before the medication is finished.

   ❑ The <u>pharmacist</u> must <u>document</u> "terminally ill" or "LTCF patient" on the prescription.

   ❑ Partial fills can be dispensed for up to <u>60 days</u> from the <u>date</u> the prescription was <u>issued</u>.

PARTIAL FILLS FOR SCHEDULE II DRUGS

SCENARIO	DEADLINE TO FILL REMAINING BALANCE
The pharmacy does not have sufficient stock of the drug	Within 72 hours after first partial filling
Requested by the patient or the practitioner who wrote the prescription	Within 30 days after issue date
Terminally ill patients or LTCF residents	Within 60 days after issue date

EMERGENCY FILLING OF SCHEDULE II DRUGS

Generally, prescribers cannot call in prescriptions for schedule II drugs. However, the DEA permits dispensing a schedule II drug pursuant to an oral prescription if the drug's immediate administration is necessary to avoid patient harm, and there is no reasonable alternative. Central fill pharmacies are prohibited from preparing emergency fills for schedule II drugs under any circumstance.

If the pharmacist is not familiar with the prescriber, they must make a good faith effort to determine that the oral prescription came from a DEA registered practitioner. This can be done by calling the prescriber using the telephone number listed in a public directory (i.e., not the number provided, as it could be fake). The pharmacist must reduce the prescription to writing immediately and it must contain all necessary information except for the prescriber's signature.

Criteria for dispensing pursuant to an oral schedule II prescription:

- Dispense the minimum necessary amount (must use professional judgement).
- Prescriber must provide the original prescription within seven days of oral authorization.

  - Original can be written or electronic.

  - Written prescription can be hand-delivered or mailed (must be postmarked by seventh day).

  - Face of the original must include the statement "Authorization for Emergency Dispensing" and the date of the oral prescription.

- Pharmacist must attach the written prescription to the emergency oral prescription.

  - Electronic prescriptions: must annotate the electronic prescription record with the emergency authorization and the date of the oral order.

- If the original prescription is not received, the pharmacist must report to the California Bureau of Narcotic Enforcement within 144 hours and must also report to the local DEA office.[219, 220]

SCHEDULE III – V PRESCRIPTIONS

Schedule V drugs can be refilled up to six months from the date of issue. There is no refill or day supply limit as long as the refills are authorized by the prescriber.[221]

Schedule III and IV prescriptions can be refilled up to five times within six months of the date written, but the total of all refills dispensed cannot exceed a 120-day supply.[222] The original fill does not count as a refill towards the 120-day supply limit. For example, if a prescription for a schedule III drug is written as "Take 1 tablet by mouth daily, #30 tablets, 5 refills", the patient can receive an initial fill of 30 tablets and up to four refills of 30 tablets each (for a 120-day supply, not counting the original fill).

---

219 H&SC 11167(d)
220 https://www.deadiversion.usdoj.gov/21cfr/cfr/1306/1306_11.htm (accessed 2020 Nov 13)
221 H&SC 11166
222 H&SC 11200

RECORDKEEPING REQUIREMENTS FOR SCHEDULE III – V REFILLS

A pharmacy can use one of the two systems for storage and retrieval of prescription refill information of schedule III and IV controlled substances:

- Paper recordkeeping system:
  - For each refill dispensed, the pharmacist must notate on the back of the prescription his or her initials, the date dispensed and the quantity dispensed. If the amount dispensed is not notated for each refill, it is assumed that the pharmacist dispensed a refill for the full refill amount.

- Electronic recordkeeping system:
  - A daily, hard copy printout of refills for controlled substances with the <u>date</u> and <u>signature</u> of <u>all the pharmacists</u> involved with the dispensing. This signifies that the pharmacists agree that the printout is correct and that is what they refilled for the day. The printout must be provided to the pharmacy within <u>72 hours</u> of the date the refill was dispensed.
  - A bound logbook or separate file documenting each day's refills. Each dispensing pharmacist during the shift signs a statement saying that what they dispensed is listed correctly.

PARTIAL FILLS OF SCHEDULE III – V PRESCRIPTIONS

Partial fills for refills of schedule III – V controlled substances are permitted if it is recorded in the same manner as a refill and if the total quantity dispensed in all of the fills does not exceed the total quantity prescribed. No dispensing can occur beyond <u>six months</u> from the date of issue. Partial fills are <u>not considered refills</u>. For example, a patient is prescribed *Ultram* #60, with two refills. This is equivalent to 180 tablets to be dispensed over a six-month period from the date of issue. Theoretically, the patient could come into the pharmacy every day for 90 days and receive two tablets.

EMERGENCY FILLING OF SCHEDULE III – V DRUGS

As discussed in the Pharmacy Practice Part 1 chapter, emergency refills without the prescriber's authorization is allowed for non-scheduled and schedule III – V drugs if the prescriber is unavailable to authorize the refill and if, in the pharmacist's judgment, failure to refill the drug could cause significant harm. The pharmacist must attempt to contact the prescriber.

TRANSFERRING CONTROLLED SUBSTANCES PRESCRIPTIONS

Schedule II prescriptions cannot be transferred. Prescriptions for <u>schedule III, IV and V drugs</u> can be transferred <u>one time only</u>, by <u>two licensed pharmacists</u>. The only exception is if the pharmacies share a "real-time, online database of the patients" (e.g., pharmacy stores in the same chain). With this type of database, pharmacies can transfer as many times as there are available refills.

For the transferring pharmacy, the prescription hard copy is pulled and "void" is written on the face (front side) of the prescription. For the receiving pharmacy, the prescription is reduced to writing by the pharmacist and "transfer" is written on the face of the transferred prescription.

The DEA number of each pharmacy must be recorded and all other information is recorded as required (see the Pharmacy Practice Part 1 chapter). Alternatively, the required information can be documented electronically. Records must be kept for <u>three years</u>.

WARNING LABELS FOR CONTROLLED SUBSTANCES

CALIFORNIA LABEL REQUIREMENTS

The following auxiliary labels are highlighted by the board as important warnings for safety and addiction prevention:

- *Opioid. Risk of overdose and addiction*. Flag/label required on outpatient containers.

- *Impaired ability to operate a vehicle or vessel*. Label required.[223]

- *Substantial risk when drug is taken in combination with alcohol*. Label required.[224]

DEA-REQUIRED WARNING STATEMENT

The following warning MUST appear on the prescription label for schedule II, III and IV drugs:

"CAUTION: Federal law prohibits the transfer of this drug to any person other than the person for whom it was prescribed."

This statement is not required on schedule V drug labels.

See the <u>Auxiliary Labels</u> chapter to review drugs that require this labeling.

DISPENSING AND DELIVERING CONTROLLED SUBSTANCES TO PATIENTS

If a controlled substance prescription is orally or electronically transmitted, the patient or the patient's representative must provide <u>proof of identify</u> to pick up the medication if he or she is <u>unknown to the pharmacy</u> staff.[225]

The United States Postal Services (USPS) permits pharmacies to mail controlled substances, with two requirements:[226]

- The prescription is placed in a plain outer container or securely wrapped in plain paper.

- The prescription label contains the name and address of the pharmacy, practitioner or other person dispensing the prescription.

Most other delivery services use the same requirements as USPS; only the USPS is mentioned by name in the DEA's requirements for mailing controlled substances.

---

223   CCR 1744
224   CCR 1744
225   B&PC 4075
226   Publication 52, Hazardous, Restricted, and Perishable Mail, § 453.4

TREATMENT OF OPIOID DEPENDENCE

OPIOID TREATMENT PROGRAMS

Approximately one million Americans are addicted to heroin and other opioids, including prescription drugs such as oxycodone, hydromorphone and hydrocodone.[227] Patients with addiction are more likely to suffer from mental health problems and be co-infected with HIV, hepatitis and sexually transmitted infections. Treating addiction can save lives and reduce healthcare costs.

Methadone is an effective schedule II drug used to treat opioid dependence, but it must be dispensed and administered through a registered opioid treatment program (OTP).[228] The methadone 40 mg soluble tablet is only FDA-approved for treating opioid addiction; the lower doses are indicated for the treatment of pain and opioid dependence.

Clinics must register with the DEA using DEA Form 363 in order to operate as an OTP. In addition to registering with the DEA, a practitioner must obtain approval and certification by the Center for Substance Abuse Treatment (CSAT). Once registered with the required parties, an OTP can dispense and administer methadone for the treatment of opioid dependence. An OTP practitioner cannot prescribe methadone, meaning they cannot provide patients with a methadone prescription for dispensing at a retail pharmacy. Likewise, when used for the treatment of opioid dependence, methadone can only be dispensed by an OTP.

In general, patients must visit an OTP every day to receive a supervised dose of methadone. There are instances when patients can receive take-home doses for self-administration. A single take-home dose can be provided for a day the OTP clinic is closed (e.g., Sundays or State and Federal holidays). Patients can also receive a take-home supply in increasing quantities over time if they are deemed eligible.[229]

METHADONE TAKE-HOME SUPPLY DISPENSING RESTRICTIONS

- First 90 days (days 1 – 90): can receive up to one take-home dose per week
- Second 90 days (days 91 – 180): can receive up to two take-home doses per week
- Third 90 days (days 181 – 270): can receive up to three take-home doses per week
- Treatment beyond 270 days and less than one year (days 270 – 364): can receive a maximum six-day supply of take-home medication
- After one year: can receive a maximum two-week supply
- After two years: can receive a maximum one-month supply of take-home medication, but must have monthly visits

---

227   http://www.cdc.gov/drugoverdose/pdf/hhs_prescription_drug_abuse_report_09.2013.pdf (accessed 2020 Nov 13)
228   42 CFR § 8.12
229   https://www.ecfr.gov/cgi-bin/retrieveECFR?gp=&SID=0d945f6e5f6068b536698ccc72159bc8&r=PART&n=42y1.0.1.1.10#se42.1.8_112 (accessed 2020 Nov 13)

OPIOID DEPENDENCE TREATMENT IN AN OFFICE-BASED SETTING

Despite the option for treatment at OTPs, opioid abuse and dependence continue to be an increasing problem. In an effort to reduce opioid addiction and improve access to care, several regulations have been passed since 2000 that expand the treatment of opioid-use disorder to office-based settings.

- **Drug Addiction Treatment Act of 2000 (DATA 2000)**
  - Permits qualified <u>physicians</u> to treat opioid dependence with narcotic medications (e.g., <u>buprenorphine</u>) in an <u>office-based setting</u>.
  - Requires completion of specific training to become a "<u>DATA-waived practitioner</u>."
  - Assigns a DATA 2000 waiver <u>unique identification number</u> (UIN); the UIN is the same as their DEA number except an "<u>X</u>" replaces the first letter.
  - Limits the number of patients the physician can treat for opioid addiction at a time to <u>30 patients</u> in the <u>first year</u> and with potential eligibility to treat <u>100 patients</u> after the first year.

- **Comprehensive Addiction and Recovery Act (CARA) of 2016**
  - Expanded DATA-waived practitioners to include qualified <u>nurse practitioners</u> (NPs) and <u>physician assistants</u> (PAs).
  - Authorized NPs and PAs can prescribe buprenorphine for a five-year period.

- **Substance Use-Disorder Prevention that Promotes Opioid Recovery and Treatment (SUPPORT) for Patients and Communities Act of 2018**
  - Granted NPs and PAs <u>permanent prescribing</u> authority of buprenorphine for opioid addiction.
  - Expanded DATA-waived practitioners to include <u>qualified clinical nurse specialists</u>, <u>certified registered nurse anesthetists</u> and <u>certified nurse midwives</u> (only eligible to prescribe buprenorphine until October 1, 2023).
  - Expanded the eligibility to treat up to <u>100 patients</u> at a time in the <u>first year</u> as a DATA-waived practitioner.
  - Allows eligible practitioners to apply to increase the treatment limit to <u>275 patients</u> after treating 100 patients for one year.

These regulations allow DATA-waived practitioners to <u>prescribe and dispense</u> schedule III − V drugs that are FDA-approved for treating opioid addiction. DATA-waived practitioners <u>do not</u> need to register as an OTP. Prescriptions for treating opioid dependence must contain the prescriber's <u>UIN and DEA number</u>. Pharmacists can verify a prescriber's DATA waiver online to determine the validity of a prescription.[230]

A practitioner <u>without</u> a DATA waiver may <u>administer</u> (but not prescribe) a <u>one-day supply</u> of medication at a time to a patient while arranging the proper referral to an opioid treatment program. This can be done for up to <u>72 hours</u> and cannot be extended.

Buprenorphine for Opioid Dependence

Buprenorphine-containing products are schedule III drugs available in various formulations. The prescribing requirements differ based on the indication for use. The combination of buprenorphine and naloxone is only FDA-approved for treating opioid dependence. Prescribers do not need a DATA waiver to prescribe <u>buprenorphine</u> products for <u>treating pain</u>, but they must specify the <u>indication</u> on the prescription.

BUPRENORPHINE: INDICATION-DEPENDENT REQUIREMENTS

INDICATION	PRESCRIBING REQUIREMENTS	FDA-APPROVED FORMULATIONS
Opioid Addiction	Prescriber must have DATA waiver ("X" in DEA number)	Buprenorphine: *Probuphine, Sublocade* Buprenorphine/naloxone: <u>*Suboxone*</u>, *Bunavail, Zubsolv*
Pain Management	Prescriber must specify the prescription is indicated for pain	Buprenorphine: <u>*Butrans*</u>, *Belbuca, Buprenex*

PRODUCTS WITH RESTRICTED SALES

Some drugs legally classified as OTC by the FDA are stored behind-the-counter (BTC) so that customers must ask the pharmacist or another staff member to retrieve the drug. The sale of some BTC drugs, such as pseudoephedrine, must be documented.

PSEUDOEPHEDRINE, EPHEDRINE, PHENYLPROPANOLAMINE AND NORPSEUDOEPHEDRINE

<u>Pseudoephedrine, ephedrine</u>, phenylpropanolamine and norpseudoephedrine-containing products have restricted distribution because they can be used to make illicit drugs, including methamphetamine and amphetamine. The <u>Combat Methamphetamine Epidemic Act (CMEA)</u> was passed in 2005 to limit the widespread availability of these precursor drugs, thereby reducing the production of methamphetamine. The CMEA and state laws apply to all four products, though they primarily control the sale of pseudoephedrine and ephedrine. Pseudoephedrine is a popular <u>decongestant</u> that is available in many single and combination cold products. Phenylephrine is an alternative OTC product that works similarly to pseudoephedrine, but cannot be used in the manufacture of amphetamine or methamphetamine. For this reason, phenylephrine does not have any OTC sales restrictions.

DRUG	NOTES
Pseudoephedrine (e.g., *Sudafed*)	In many cough and cold products
Ephedrine (ingredient in *Bronkaid, Primatene*)	For asthma symptom relief (not guideline recommended)
Norpseudoephedrine	Not available in the U.S.
Phenylpropanolamine	By prescription only for veterinary use

Requirements for OTC Sales

Pseudoephedrine, ephedrine and their transaction logbook must be kept behind the counter or in a locked cabinet. They are typically kept in the pharmacy, but do not need to be as long as a customer cannot access them without assistance from a store employee. All sales should be recorded, with the customer signing the logbook. The exception to this requirement is the purchase of a single-dose package of pseudoephedrine, which contains a maximum of 60 mg (two 30 mg tablets).

Maximum Limits for OTC Sales

The daily and monthly limits for ephedrine and pseudoephedrine sales are derived from the base amount of drug. For example, pseudoephedrine hydrochloride 30 mg tablets contain 24.6 mg of pseudoephedrine base. Therefore, an individual can purchase a maximum of 146 pseudoephedrine hydrochloride 30 mg tablets in one day (3,600 mg maximum pseudoephedrine base per day / 24.6 mg pseudoephedrine base per tablet = 146 tablets).

MAXIMUM LIMITS FOR OTC SALES

Quantity limits for OTC sales of pseudoephedrine and ephedrine:

- 3.6 grams per day
- 9 grams in a 30-day period
- 7.5 grams in a 30-day period for each mail-order purchase
- 3 packages per transaction

These limits are for OTC sales only. A larger quantity can be dispensed with a valid prescription.

Purchase Requirements for OTC Sales

All pharmacies that sell ephedrine or pseudoephedrine products must "self-certify" to the Attorney General of the United States that they are trained in the sales regulations for these drugs. Purchase requirements include:

- Documentation of the customer name, address, date and time of sale and signature in the logbook

- Photo identification issued by the state or federal government (e.g., driver's license, passport, state identification card)[231]

- Verification of customer identity by the store staff

- Documentation of the product name and quantity sold

The DEA requires that the logbook be kept in a secure location for at least two years. Information in the logbook cannot be shared with the public.

DEXTROMETHORPHAN

Dextromethorphan is an OTC cough suppressant used in more than 120 cough and cold medications, either as a single agent or in combination with other drugs. It is often abused in high doses (especially by teenagers and young adults) to generate euphoria and visual and auditory hallucinations. Illicit use of dextromethorphan is often referred to as "robo-tripping" or "skittling." Dextromethorphan is not currently scheduled under the Controlled Substances Act (CSA), but the DEA has indicated that dextromethorphan may become a scheduled drug in the future.

231   https://www.deadiversion.usdoj.gov/meth/alternate_ID2.pdf (accessed 2020 Nov 13)

Dextromethorphan-containing products cannot be sold to anyone under 18 years old without a prescription in California. The purchaser must provide government-issued identification (with name, date of birth, description and picture of the purchaser), unless the pharmacy staff reasonably believes that the purchaser looks at least 25 years old. Dextromethorphan products can be kept on the floor shelves outside of the pharmacy area with other OTC products, and the cashier staff can check for the age requirement.

HYPODERMIC NEEDLES AND SYRINGES

A pharmacist can furnish hypodermic needles and syringes to patients without a prescription in the following situations:[232]

- The pharmacist knows the patient and the pharmacist has previously been provided with a prescription or other proof of legitimate medical need for the needles and syringes (e.g., administering insulin).

- To a person 18 years of age or older as a public health measure to prevent the transmission of HIV, viral hepatitis and other bloodborne diseases among persons who use syringes and hypodermic needles, and to prevent subsequent infection of sexual partners, newborn children or other persons. There is no limit on the number of needles and syringes that can be provided.

- Use for animals, as long as the animal's owner is known to the pharmacist or the person's identity can be properly established.

- For industrial use, as determined by the board.

Pharmacies that sell syringes without a prescription must:

- Store needles and syringes in a manner that ensures that they are not accessible to unauthorized persons.

- Provide for the safe disposal of needles and syringes:
    - Sell or furnish sharps containers or mail-back sharps containers.
    - Provide on-site sharps collection and disposal (pharmacies can take back used syringes only if enclosed in a sharps container).

- Provide written or verbal information to customers at the time of sale on how to access drug addiction treatment or testing and treatment for HIV and HCV, and information about how to safely dispose of sharps waste.

---

232 B&PC 4145.5

CHAPTER 8

AUXILIARY LABELS

AUXILIARY LABELS

Auxiliary labels are placed on the container and alert the patient to key warnings, dietary requirements and storage or administration requirements. For example, drugs with central nervous system (CNS) depressant effects can slow down reaction time and subsequently cause motor vehicle accidents. To increase public awareness on the side effects of certain drugs and to reduce driving under the influence, the board has mandated a warning label that states "Do not drive a car or operate heavy machinery while using this medicine" for select drugs.

Auxiliary labels should be evidence-based and written in simple language. They should be placed in a standard location on the label and should be provided for each prescription in which the use is appropriate, rather than at the discretion of the pharmacist. This list contains select auxiliary labels used in dispensing medications. It should not be considered exhaustive, but it does represent major categories of labels.

AUXILIARY LABELS: KEY WARNINGS

LABEL	COMMENT
CAUTION: Federal Law PROHIBITS the transfer of this drug to any person other than the patient for whom it was prescribed.	<u>Federal law requires</u> that schedule II, III and IV drugs must have the following warning: "Caution: Federal law prohibits the transfer of this drug to any person other than the patient for whom it was prescribed."
CAUTION: OPIOID. RISK OF OVERDOSE AND ADDICTION. *	<u>State law requirement</u> for drugs that contain single or combination opioids. All opioid prescription bottles must contain the notice, "Caution: Opioid. Risk of overdose and addiction." This is in addition to the cautionary statement required by federal law for schedule II, III and IV drugs (see previous entry). See opioid list in Controlled Substances Part 1 chapter.

LABEL	COMMENT
CAUTION: Do not take with alcohol or nonprescribed drugs without consulting your doctor.	State law requirement to include for drugs that cannot be taken with alcohol. The following classes of drugs pose a substantial risk when taken in combination with alcohol. A pharmacist must include a warning on the prescription label for the following drugs:[233] ■ Disulfiram and other drugs (e.g., chlorpropamide, metronidazole, tinidazole) which may cause a disulfiram-like reaction (avoid alcohol for 48 hours after last dose) ■ Monoamine oxidase inhibitors ■ Nitrates ■ Cycloserine ■ Antidiabetic agents including insulin, metformin and sulfonylureas (due to risk of hypoglycemia) ■ Any other drug which, based upon a pharmacist's professional judgment, may pose a substantial risk when taken in combination with alcohol. Includes opioids (all, but specific warning for *Kadian, Zohydro ER, Opana,** Nucynta ER*), tramadol, benzodiazepines, barbiturates, non-benzodiazepine hypnotics (e.g., zolpidem), anticonvulsants, antipsychotics, some antidepressants, skeletal muscle relaxants.
 May cause DROWSINESS USE CARE when operating a car or dangerous machinery.	State law requirement to include for drugs that can impair a person's ability to drive or operate machinery. The following drug classes require a warning on the prescription label of the drug container:[234] ■ Muscle relaxants and analgesics with CNS depressant effects ■ Antipsychotic drugs with CNS depressant effects ■ Antidepressants with CNS depressant effects (e.g., mirtazapine, trazodone) ■ Antihistamines, motion sickness drugs, antipruritics, antiemetics, anticonvulsants and antihypertensive drugs with CNS depressant effects ■ All narcotics and controlled substances (schedules II – V) with CNS depressant effects (e.g., hypnotics) ■ Anticholinergic drugs that may impair vision ■ Any other drug which, based on the pharmacist's professional judgment, may impair a patient's ability to operate a vehicle or vessel (e.g., dopamine agonists such as ropinirole)
 DO NOT TAKE THIS DRUG IF YOU BECOME PREGNANT	Patients should be advised not to use these drugs during pregnancy or breastfeeding. This may be due to risk of fetal injury, teratogenicity or other exposure-related concerns. ■ ACE inhibitors, renin inhibitors ■ Valproic acid, carbamazepine ■ Angiotensin II receptor blockers ■ Phenytoin, phenobarbital ■ Statins ■ Lithium, topiramate ■ Warfarin ■ NSAIDs ■ Hormones (most, including estradiol, progesterone, raloxifene, testosterone, contraceptives) ■ Ribavirin ■ Misoprostol, methotrexate ■ Isotretinoin and topical retinoids ■ Leflunomide, lenalidomide, thalidomide ■ Paroxetine ■ Dutasteride, finasteride

**Brand discontinued but name still used in practice.

233   CCR 1744(b)
234   CCR 1744(a)

Labels courtesy of shamrocklabels
*©RxPrep, Inc.

LABEL	COMMENT
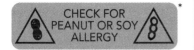	Check for <u>peanut or soy allergy</u>. Includes progesterone (*Prometrium* only, not other formulations), clevidipine (*Cleviprex*) and propofol.
 **For further discussion of high-alert medications refer to the RxPrep NAPLEX Course Book. Additional clinical knowledge of these medications is <u>required</u> for CPJE.**	The <u>Institute for Safe Medication Practices (ISMP)</u> defines <u>high-alert medications</u> as those that have high risk of causing <u>significant patient harm</u> when they are used in error. Safeguards must be put in place to reduce the risk of errors, including the proper use of labeling. **High-alert medications include:** ■ **Adrenergic agonists** (e.g., epinephrine) – specify drug dose in milligrams. Note that epinephrine 1:1,000 is 1 mg/mL and 1:10,000 is 0.1 mg/mL. ■ **Adrenergic antagonists** (e.g., beta-blockers) – caution when converting from PO to IV. High risk for error due to differences in bioavailability. ■ **Sedatives** [e.g., midazolam (*Versed*), propofol (*Diprivan*)] – these are common ICU medications used to keep patients comfortable on ventilators. Respiratory rate and mental status must be closely monitored. ■ **Antiarrhythmics** (e.g., amiodarone, sotalol) – to be administered by protocol that defines dose or infusion rate and requirement for cardiac (ECG) monitoring. ■ **Anticoagulants** (e.g., heparin, argatroban, warfarin) – to be administered by protocol that includes required baseline labs (e.g., INR, aPTT, CBC), states lab goals (indication based), frequency of monitoring labs and dose/rate adjustments based on lab values. Protocol should also include monitoring for symptoms of bleeding and reversal strategy. ■ **Insulin** – to be administered by protocol that includes initial infusion rate (for IV administration), blood glucose (BG) and potassium monitoring frequency, rate adjustment based on BG and when to notify physician. ■ **Positive inotropes** (e.g., dobutamine, milrinone) – prior to administration and frequently during administration monitor BP, HR, hemodynamic parameters (if available) and urine output. ■ **Opioids** (e.g., hydromorphone, fentanyl) – screen and monitor patients at risk for oversedation and respiratory depression. A conversion support system should be used to help convert between agents. Use tall man lettering and separate look-alike/sound-alike agents. ■ **Electrolytes** (e.g., hypertonic saline, potassium) – to be administered by protocol with a maximum infusion rate and monitoring requirements. Should not be prepared on the patient unit.
HIGH ALERT! Paralytic Paralytic Paralytic Paralytic	<u>Neuromuscular blocking agents</u> (cisatracurium, vecuronium, succinylcholine, rocuronium, pancuronium) can <u>only</u> be given to a patient who is already on BOTH an <u>analgesic</u> (e.g., fentanyl) and under <u>deep sedation</u> (e.g., propofol, midazolam) with pain and sedation assessed continuously.
IMPORTANT FINISH **ALL THIS MEDICATION** UNLESS OTHERWISE DIRECTED BY PRESCRIBER	These medications can have serious clinical implications if discontinued before the course has been completed (e.g., antimicrobial resistance or not fully treating an infection with antibiotics, antifungals or antivirals).
 **MAY CAUSE BLURRED VISION**	Medications that are well known to cause <u>blurry vision</u> include anticholinergics (e.g., scopolamine), voriconazole (*Vfend*), telithromycin and PDE-5 inhibitors (e.g., sildenafil). Alcohol and CNS depressants can cause blurry or double vision (diplopia) if toxic. Digoxin can cause yellow/green halos if toxic. Other drugs that can affect vision include: hydroxychloroquine, tamoxifen, amiodarone, ethambutol, isotretinoin, isoniazid and ivabradine. Refer to the RxPrep NAPLEX Course Book for details.

LABEL	COMMENT
AVOID PROLONGED **EXPOSURE TO SUNLIGHT** WHILE TAKING THIS MEDICATION	Avoid prolonged exposure to direct and/or artificial sunlight while using these medications due to increased <u>skin sensitivity</u>. ■ Sulfa antibiotics　　■ Ritonavir and a few other HIV drugs ■ Quinolones, tetracyclines　　■ NSAIDs (piroxicam, diclofenac, ibuprofen, naproxen) ■ Metronidazole, isoniazid ■ Topical retinoids (newer ones less risk), isotretinoin (oral)　　■ Diuretics
When taking this medication the effectiveness of birth control pills are decreased. Use additional and/or alernative methods of birth control. *	It is important to counsel the patient that they will need to use an alternative form of contraception to prevent unwanted pregnancy while taking this medication as it may make <u>birth control pills less effective</u>. ■ Barbiturates (e.g., phenobarbital)　　■ Anticonvulsants (topiramate, lamotrigine, carbamazepine, primidone, phenytoin, oxcarbazepine) ■ St. John's wort ■ Ampicillin, tetracycline ■ Rifampin, rifapentine, griseofulvin　　■ Some HIV drugs (some protease inhibitors, NNRTIs) ■ Bosentan
WARNING: If your stool becomes soft and watery after using this antibiotic, contact your doctor immediately. *	<u>Persistent diarrhea</u> due to colitis may occur weeks after using the medication. This should be reported to your doctor immediately as it can be a dangerous side effect. Includes clindamycin, quinolones and broad-spectrum antibiotics.
MAY CAUSE **DISCOLORATION** OF THE URINE OF FECES	May cause <u>discoloration of the urine, skin and sweat</u>. May stain contact lenses and clothing. ■ Entacapone, carbidopa/levodopa　　■ Sulfasalazine ■ Metronidazole, rifampin　　■ Doxorubicin, mitoxantrone ■ Nitrofurantoin, phenazopyridine　　■ Propofol

AUXILIARY LABELS: DIETARY REQUIREMENTS

LABEL	COMMENT
TAKE MEDICATION ON AN **EMPTY STOMACH** 1 HOUR BEFORE OR 2 TO 3 HOURS AFTER A MEAL UNLESS OTHERWISE DIRECTED BY YOUR DOCTOR. *	These medications are to be taken on an <u>empty stomach</u>. While 1 hour before or 2-3 hours after a meal is a standard time frame, individual medications may differ. ■ Ampicillin, Voriconazole (*Vfend*)　　■ Levothyroxine ■ Efavirenz (*Sustiva/Atripla*), didanosine (*Videx*)　　■ Oxymorphone (*Opana***) ■ Bisphosphonates　　■ Mycophenolate (*CellCept*), tacrolimus extended release (*Astagraf XL, Envarsus XR*) ■ Captopril ■ Iron (if tolerated), PPIs　　■ Zafirlukast
TAKE WITH **FOOD**	These medications are to be taken <u>with food</u>. ■ Carvedilol (*Coreg*), metoprolol tartrate (*Lopressor*)　　■ Metformin (IR with breakfast and dinner, XR with dinner) ■ Lovastatin (with dinner)　　■ Itraconazole capsules ■ Fenofibrate and derivatives (*Lipofen, Fenoglide*)　　■ Phosphate binders (when eating) 　　■ NSAIDs, steroids ■ Niacin, gemfibrozil (*Lopid*)　　■ Opioids (except *Opana***)

*Brand discontinued but name still used in practice.

LABEL	COMMENT
 MEDICATION SHOULD BE TAKEN WITH PLENTY OF **WATER**	Drugs can get "stuck" going down, especially if dysphagia is present. It is preferable to take most with a <u>full glass of water</u>. Includes sulfamethoxazole/trimethoprim (*Bactrim*), bisphosphonates, sulfasalazine (*Azulfidine* – take with water & food) and pancrelipase.
AVOID TAKING THIS MEDICATION WITH GRAPEFRUIT OR GRAPEFRUIT JUICE. *	Do <u>not</u> eat <u>grapefruit</u> or drink grapefruit juice at any time while using this medicine. ■ Lovastatin, simvastatin, atorvastatin ■ Cyclosporine, tacrolimus ■ Amiodarone, dofetilide ■ Diazepam, triazolam ■ Buspirone, carbamazepine ■ Verapamil, nicardipine, felodipine, nisoldipine and nifedipine
 DO NOT TAKE DAIRY PRODUCTS ANTACID OR IRON PREPARATIONS WITHIN ONE HOUR OF THIS MEDICATION	<u>Separate</u> from <u>dairy products, calcium, magnesium, iron and antacids</u> because it can make the medication less effective. Includes tetracyclines, quinolones and levothyroxine.

AUXILIARY LABELS: STORAGE OR ADMINISTRATION REQUIREMENTS

Many of these medications will require further clinical knowledge. Several of these concepts can be found in the Learning IV Medications chapter in the RxPrep NAPLEX Course Book.

LABEL	COMMENT
SHAKE WELL	Used for medications that may not have an equal distribution of drug unless shaken due to separation or alternative factors. This includes all <u>suspensions</u>, most asthma aerosol inhalers, nasal steroid sprays and lidocaine viscous topical liquid.
SWALLOW WHOLE DO NOT CRUSH BREAK OR CHEW	<u>Do not chew or crush</u> as this can alter the effects of the medication and be dangerous. Swallow whole. Enteric coated formulations (e.g., bisacodyl, aspirin), any drug that ends with XR, ER, LA, SR, CR, CRT, SA, TR, TD or has 24 in the name, or the ending "–cont" (for controlled release, such as *MS Contin* or *Oxycontin*) and timecaps and sprinkles. Note: can cut metoprolol extended-release and carbidopa/levodopa SR at the score line (for half the dose), but cannot crush or chew.
 **CHEMOTHERAPY DRUG TOXIC** Dispose of as BIO-HAZARD	Chemotherapeutic agents require special packaging and labeling for proper handling of the medication and proper disposal of the bag and tubing. (Alternative wording is Chemotherapy: Dispose of Properly.)
FOR IRRIGATION ONLY NOT FOR IV USE	Any type of irrigation should be labeled so that it is NOT administered intravenously. This includes peritoneal dialysis irrigation solution, saline and sterile water irrigation solution.
 **EPIDURAL**	Epidural or intrathecal solutions should be labeled to decrease risk of administration via an incorrect route.
DO NOT REFRIGERATE	Remember: Dear Sweet Pharmacist, Freezing Makes Me Edgy! **(DSPFMME)** **D**exmedetomidine, **S**ulfamethoxazole/Trimethoprim, **P**henytoin, **F**urosemide, **M**etronidazole, **M**oxifloxacin, **E**noxaparin

📷 *Labels courtesy of* shamrock labels
📷 *©RxPrep, Inc.*

LABEL	COMMENT
REFRIGERATE *	These medications must be kept <u>refrigerated</u> (i.e., between 36-46°F). They should not be kept frozen or at room temperature. **Antibiotic suspensions (refrigerate after reconstitution):** amoxicillin/clavulanate *(Augmentin)*, amoxicillin (refrigeration not required, but improves taste), cefpodoxime, cefprozil, cefuroxime *(Ceftin)*, ceftibuten, cephalexin *(Keflex)*, erythromycin/benzoyl peroxide gel *(Benzamycin)*, penicillin V **Eyedrops:** latanoprost *(Xalatan – unopened)*, tafluprost *(Zioptan – unopened)* **Others:** adalimumab *(Humira)*, dronabinol *(Marinol, Syndros)*, etanercept *(Enbrel)*, calcitonin nasal *(Miacalcin)*, ESAs *(Epogen, Aranesp, Procrit)*, etoposide *(VePesid)*, filgrastim *(Neupogen)*, insulins (that patient is not using), interferons (all), lopinavir/ritonavir solution *(Kaletra)*, alprostadil *(Muse, Caverject)*, ritonavir soft gel capsule *(Norvir)*, octreotide *(Sandostatin)*, sirolimus solution *(Rapamune)*, teriparatide *(Forteo)*, thyrolar *(Liotrix)*, lactobacillus *(Visbiome)*, NuvaRing (prior to dispensing, patient can keep at room temp), promethazine suppositories, typhoid oral capsules *(Vivotif)*, formoterol (prior to dispensing, patient can keep at room temp), dornase alfa *(Pulmozyme)*
PROTECT FROM LIGHT *	Remember: Protect Every Necessary Med from Daylight **(PENMD)** **P**hytonadione, **E**poprostenol, **N**itroprusside, **M**icafungin, **D**oxycycline
 FOR EXTERNAL USE **ONLY**	For <u>external use only</u> (topicals), may require: "For the Eye," "For the Ear," "For the Nose," "For Rectal Use Only," "For Vaginal Use Only," "Not to be Taken by Mouth."
ADMINISTER BY INTRAMUSCULAR (IM) INJECTION *	Intramuscular (IM) injections should be labeled to decrease the risk of administration via an incorrect route. For example, the preferred route of promethazine injection is IM due to risk of tissue irritation and damage. It is contraindicated to give promethazine via subcutaneous injection, and not recommended to administer IV. Contraindicated in patients < 2 years old due to risk of fatal respiratory depression.
FOR CENTRAL LINE ADMINISTRATION ONLY *	For drugs that must be administered via <u>central</u> (not peripheral) IV access only. Due primarily to the risk of phlebitis (vein irritation) and for vesicant medications (risk of severe tissue damage if line extravasates). **Risk of phlebitis** ■ Parenteral nutrition, most chemotherapeutics ■ Calcium chloride, hypertonic saline, mannitol, digoxin ■ Foscarnet, nafcillin, mitomycin ■ Quinupristin/dalfopristin *(Synercid)*, KCl, amiodarone (concentrated) **Vesicants** ■ Vasopressors (e.g., norepinephrine, dopamine) ■ Anthracyclines (e.g., doxorubicin) ■ Vinca alkaloids (e.g., vincristine) ■ Do not administer vincristine by intrathecal administration.
 **FILTER**	Remember: That's my **GAL, PLAT** **G**olimumab, **A**miodarone, **L**orazepam, **P**henytoin, **L**ipids, **A**mphotericin B, **T**axanes

Labels courtesy of shamrocklabels
*©RxPrep, Inc.

INDEX

Study Tips

Adulteration vs. Misbranding 22

Advantages of CSOS 108

Buprenorphine: Indication-Dependent Requirements 132

Considerations to Determine if Loss or Theft is Significant 110

Controlled Substance Schedule Definitions 95

DEA Forms for Managing Controlled Substances 102

DEA-Required Warning Statement 129

Determining the Validity of a DEA Number 118

Drug Recall Classifications 24

Exemptions to C-R Packaging 40

Federal Law Requirements for Prescription Labels 38

First Letter of DEA Number for Each Registrant Type 117

Maximum Limits for OTC Sales 133

Medi-Cal Prescription Form Requirements 34

Methadone Take-Home Supply Dispensing Restrictions 130

Mid-Level Practitioner Prescribing Authority 116

NABP "Red Flags" of Diversion 119

Paper Versus Electronic Ordering 103

Partial Fills for Schedule II Drugs 126

Pharmacist Supervision Limits 9

Protected Health Information (PHI) 49

Select Self-Diagnosable Conditions and Treatment Options 77

The FDA's Flush List 26

Triplicate Form 222 for Schedule II Drug Transactions 105

Using the Orange Book 51

Numbers

503A 63

503B 64

A

Accreditation Council for Pharmacy Education (ACPE) 7

Adulteration 22

Advanced Practice Pharmacist (APh) 10

Advisory Committee on Immunization Practices (ACIP) 68

Aid-in-Dying: *See* Death with Dignity

Antimicrobial Stewardship Programs 87

Automated Dispensing Cabinet (ADC) 58

Automated Drug Delivery Systems (ADDS) 58

Auxiliary Labels 129, 135

    Dietary Requirements 138

    Key Warnings 135

    Storage or Administration Requirements 139

B

Barbiturate Schedules 98

Barcoding 62

Basic Life Support 68

Behind The Counter (BTC) 132

Biologics 54, 67

Biosimilars 54

Blood Clotting Products 57

Blood Pressure 75, 81

Board of Pharmacy 6

Body Fat Analysis 84

Bone Density Screening 85

Buprenorphine 131, 132

C

California Bureau of Narcotic Enforcement 127

California Immunization Registry 68

California Security Form 34, 120, 123

Cannabidiol (CBD) 99, 100

Cannabis 99, 100

Center for Substance Abuse Treatment (CSAT) 130

Centers for Disease Control and Prevention (CDC) 68, 75, 77, 78

Certified Nurse Midwife (CNM) 31

Cesamet: *See* Nabilone

Chart Order 11, 32

Child-Resistant (C-R) Packaging 40

Cholesterol Screening 85

Clinical Laboratory Improvement Amendments (CLIA) 79

Codeine Schedules 99

Collaborative Drug Therapy Management (CDTM) 10

Collaborative Practice Agreement (CPA) 10

Combat Methamphetamine Epidemic Act (CMEA) 15, 132

Compounding 61, 62, 63

Comprehensive Addiction and Recovery Act (CARA) 126, 131

Consumer Medication Information 41

Continuing Education (CE) 8, 10, 16

Controlled Substance

    Authorized to Prescribe 116

    Cancelling or Voiding Order 110

    Delivering 129

    Dispensing 129

    Emergency Filling 128

    Inventory Requirements 17

    Loss or Theft 110

Controlled Substance, continued

Ordering Schedule II 107

Out-Of-State Prescriptions 120

Partial Fill 128

Prescription Requirements 120

Electronic 124

Errors or Omissions 124

Faxed 123

Oral 123

Written 120

Recordkeeping 17, 128

Refills 127

Returning to Supplier or Manufacturer 112

Selling Controlled Substances 109

Sending to Reverse Distributor 112

Transferring Between Registrants 109

Transfers 128

Warning Labels 129

Controlled Substance Ordering System (CSOS) 103, 104, 108

Controlled Substances Act (CSA) 94, 100, 133

Controlled Substance Utilization Review and Evaluation System (CURES) 119

Corresponding Responsibility 118

CPJE PSI Candidate Information Bulletin 2

Current Good Manufacturing Practices (CGMPs) 64

D

Death with Dignity 58

Dentist 30, 116

Depression Screening 86

Designated Representative-In-Charge (DRIC) 7

Detailed Written Order (DWO) 19

Dextromethorphan 133, 134

Diphenhydramine 68

Dispensing During an Emergency 58

Diversion 118

Dronabinol 99

Drug Addiction Treatment Act (DATA 2000) 131

DATA 2000 Waiver 131

Drug Delivery 21

Drug Enforcement Administration (DEA) 10, 30, 94

DEA Number 102, 117, 120

DEA Registrant 103, 104

Drug Enforcement Administration (DEA) Forms

Form 41: 102, 112, 113

Form 106: 102, 110, 111

Form 222: 102, 103, 104, 108, 109, 110, 112

Lost or Stolen 108

Form 224: 102, 103, 104

Form 225: 102

Form 363: 102, 130

Form 510: 102

Drug Paraphernalia 100

Needle Sales 134

Syringe Sales 134

Drug Quality and Security Act (DQSA)

Drug Recalls 24

Drug Stock 22

Drug Storage 23

Drug Substitution 53

Drug Supply Chain Security Act (DSCSA) 20

Drug Utilization Review (DUR) 46

Durable Medical Equipment (DME) 19

E

Electronic Health Record (EHR) 67

Emergency Contraception (EC) 69, 70

Emtricitabine (FTC) 78

Ephedrine 132, 133

Epidiolex: *See* Cannabidiol (CBD)

Epinephrine 57, 68

Expiration Date 39

F

Farm Bill 100

Foreign Pharmacy Graduate Equivalency Examination (FPGEE) 11

Foreign Pharmacy Graduate Examination Committee (FPGEC) 7, 11

Formularies 54

G

Glucose Screening 84

H

Health Insurance Portability and Accountability Act (HIPAA) 49

Privacy Notice 52

Health Screenings 75, 84

Hemp 99, 100

High-Alert Medications 137

Hormonal Contraceptives 75

I

Immunization Administration 8

Immunizations 67, 68, 77

Institute for Safe Medication Practices (ISMP) 137

Instructions for Use (IFU) 41

Intern: *See* Pharmacist Intern

Internet Pharmacy 55

J

Joint Commission (TJC) 80

L

Levonorgestrel 69

M

Marijuana 94, 99, 100

Marinol: *See* Dronabinol

Medi-Cal 34, 89

Medicare 89, 90

Medicare Part D Opioid Limits 125

Medication Errors 88

Medication Guides (MedGuides) 42

Medication Order: *See* Chart Order

Medication Therapy Management (MTM) 86, 89

Medication Utilization Evaluation (MUE) 87

MedWatch 25

Methadone 130

Mid-Level Practitioner 116

Misbranding 22, 41

Mobile Pharmacy 58

N

Nabilone 99

Naloxone 31, 72, 73

National Association of Boards of Pharmacy (NABP) 2, 7

National Healthcareer Association (NHA) 12

National Patient Safety Goals 86

Naturopathic Doctor 31, 116

Nicotine Replacement Therapy (NRT) 8, 74, 75

Norpseudoephedrine 132

Notice to Consumers 49

Nurse Practitioner 31, 116, 131

O

Opioid Treatment Program (OTP) 130

Optometrist 30, 116

Outsourcing Facilities 64

P

Pain 83

Patient Counseling 46, 75

Interpretive Services 48

Mailed Prescriptions 48

Offer to Counsel 48

Patient Package Insert (PPI) 41

Patient Profile 44

Peer Review 88

Pharmacist 7

Authority to Furnish Medications 31

Breaks 9

Disciplinary Action 8

Duties 6, 7

License Renewal 8

Licensure 7

Mandatory Reporting 27

Prescribing Authority 116

Registered Pharmacist (RPh) Duties 8

Supervision 9

Pharmacist-In-Charge (PIC) 7, 103

Duties 7

Pharmacist Intern 10

Duties 6, 9, 10

Registration 11

Pharmacist's Manual 94

Pharmacists Recovery Program 12

Pharmacy

Inspection 13

Off-Site Record Storage 18

Policies and Procedures 14, 88

Recordkeeping 15, 17

Security 14

Space and Equipment 13

Pharmacy Clerk 12

Pharmacy Technician 11

Duties 6, 11

Licensure 12

Pharmacy Technician Certification Board (PTCB) 12

Pharmacy Technician Trainee 12

Pharmacy & Therapeutics (P&T) Committee 54

Phenylpropanolamine 132

Physical Assessments 80

Physician 30, 116

Physician Assistant 31, 116, 131

Podiatrist 30, 116

Poison Prevention Packaging Act (PPPA) 40

Post-Exposure Prophylaxis (PEP) 79

Power of Attorney (POA) 104

Pre-Exposure Prophylaxis (PrEP) 78, 79

Prescriber

Deceased 31

Foreign 32

Out-of-State 32

Prescribing for Family Member 31

Prescription

Converting 30-day to 90-day Supply 35

Emergency Refills 36

Errors and Omissions 34

Label Requirements 38

Refills 36

Refusal to Dispense 55

Requirements 32

Returns 25

Transfers 37

Transmission 33

Prescription Drug Monitoring Program (PDMP) 119

Protected Health Information (PHI) 49

Pseudoephedrine 132, 133

Q

Quality Assurance 66, 67, 86, 88

R

Red Flag: *See* Diversion

Repackaging 61

Blister Packs 63

Respiratory Rate 82

Reverse Distributor 26, 112

Risk Evaluation and Mitigation Strategy (REMS) 43

Root Cause Analysis (RCA) 88

S

SB 493: 67

Scheduled Drugs 94

Formulation-Specific 98

Schedule Changes 98

State-Specific 98

Schedule I 94, 95

Schedule II 95

Emergency Filling 127

Long-Term Care Facility (LTCF) 126

Multiple Prescriptions 125

Partial Filling 125

Prescriptions 125

Transfer 128

Schedule III 95, 96

Schedule IV 95, 97

Schedule V 95, 98

Scope of Practice 30

Self-Administered Hormonal Contraceptive 75

Self-Assessment Forms 7, 13, 16

Community Pharmacy and Hospital Outpatient Pharmacy Self-Assessment Form 3

Compounding Self-Assessment Form 3

Self-Prescribing 31

Shortages 23

Smoking Cessation 74

Standard Order Set 86

Star Rating 89

Substance Use-Disorder Prevention that Promotes Opioid Recovery and Treatment (SUPPORT) for Patients and Communities Act 131

Syndros: *See* Dronabinol

T

Tablet Splitting 91

Take-Back Program 26

Tamper-Resistant Security Forms 34

Tech-Check-Tech 11

Telepharmacy 56

Telephone Orders 32

Temperature 82

Tenofovir Disoproxil Fumarate (TDF) 78

Tetrahydrocannabinol (THC) 99, 100

Therapeutic Interchange 55

The Script 3

Tobacco Screening 86

Translation 40

Travel Medications 77, 78

Truvada 78, 79

U

Ulipristal 69

Unique Identification Number (UIN) 131

Unit-Dose Containers 62

Beyond-Use Date (BUD) 62

Label 62

United States Medical Eligibility Criteria (USMEC) 75

United States Pharmacopeia (USP) 63

V

Verbal Order 32

Veterinarian 30, 64, 116

Vital Sign Measurement 80

Image Credits

Some images have been modified from their original state. All images are being used for illustrative purposes only. Any person depicted in the content is a model.

Cover and book design credits –

ALPA PROD/Shutterstock

Bacho/Shutterstock

davooda/Shutterstock

Dean Drobot/Shutterstock

Flamingo Images/Shutterstock

Kzenon/Shutterstock

kurhan/Shutterstock

LightField Studios/Shutterstock

pikselstock/Shutterstock

Scott Rothstein/Shutterstock

Uranium/Shutterstock

NOTES

NOTES

NOTES